# Dedication

• • • • • • • •

*First, for Bill Soukup, my best friend and greatest fan,*
*and for my soulful Lillie and powerful Thea:  It is true - I love you more than anything.*

*Second, for my grandmother and namesake, Mary (Gibas) Kaczmarek: You saw it long before I did,*
*and I thank you and all the women of our household for loving support along the way.*

# Take Charge *of* Your Legal Career

• • • • • • • •

**Skillful Development**

5417 Eastwych Court
Charlotte, NC 28226

Printed in the United States of America

# Table of Contents

· · · · · · · ·

# Introduction

• • • • • • • •

## Now *is the* Time

Congratulations! You have picked up this Workbook and that signals a key step in your career—you have confidence and a strong footing in your substantive expertise and are ready to focus on developing business and building a practice. Taking this step is significant in many ways. The most important one is that **learning how to develop business allows you to have greater control over your career, now and in the future**. Certainly there are many factors that impact career success which are out of an individual's control. The last economic downturn is a prime example. But if you take control of variables that are subject to your influence—such as learning the discipline of building a sustaining practice—you guarantee yourself a greater degree of security and many more career-related opportunities.

*New York Times* editorial page writer Thomas Friedman commented on what he referred to as "the new untouchable," i.e., the professional who survives and thrives in his/her career because he/she has developed the skills to go beyond just "doing a job:"

> "A Washington lawyer friend recently told me about layoffs at his firm. I asked him who was getting axed. He said it was interesting: lawyers who were used to just showing up and having work handed to them were the first to go because with the bursting of the credit bubble, that flow of work just isn't there. But those who have the ability to imagine new services, new opportunities and new ways to recruit work were being retained. They are the *new untouchables*."

Learning how to build business is part of being a "new untouchable."

## Business Development *as* "Science" *and* "Art"

There is no scarcity of opportunity for developing new business. What tends to be in short supply are time, skills and focus. The *Practical Workbook* is designed to help you to use your time wisely, develop new skills, and focus your efforts for successfully developing business. The *Practical Workbook* describes the business discipline of developing client opportunities and provides you with time-tested strategies for doing so. That is the "science" part of the process. It's up to you, however, to adapt the formula to your own practice and personality style. This is the "art" of business development, and there are many variations on the theme. It makes sense to study the science and over time, to implement it in a way that is comfortable and effective for you. At first it may seem uncomfortable and awkward, but in time you'll adapt the discipline to your own personal style.

## Mindset *is* Critical

It's difficult to be motivated to do something you find to be uncomfortable or distasteful, and unfortunately that's how many lawyers view the prospect of developing business. So the first step in the business-building process is to approach it with the right mindset.

There are two important considerations to keep in mind. First, consider business development not just as a way to generate revenue or to obtain work to keep you busy, but most importantly as a conduit to obtaining more of the work you enjoy from clients who appreciate your services. Those objectives should be the ultimate goal of your efforts. Second, rather than defining business development as trying to sell someone a service they may or may not need or want, view it as being helpful to others by offering your talent and expertise to solve their important problems. In other words, business development promotes a mutually beneficial exchange of value between you and your target clients, a positive experience for both of you.

The "elephant in the room" that may impede your interest in and motivation for business development is the concept that "non-billable time" is "a waste of time." Only lawyers and law firms talk about "non-billable time" in a way that implies it is not valuable. To build a sustaining practice, an attorney **must invest non-billable time** in strategic business-building efforts. Your career is an important asset that you have earned through study, expense and perhaps some blood, sweat and tears to boot. An asset—think of your house, car, health, most important relationships, etc.—must be protected and improved to obtain the best return on investment. Investing non-billable time in strategic business development initiatives will pay dividends for the life of your career.

## Maximizing Your Use *of the* Workbook

The *Practical Workbook* is built on a format of exploring key business development concepts related to a specific theme. For example, in the section ***Understanding the Target Market's Need for Legal Services***, the discussion is followed by an exercise to reinforce the concept. Each exercise is designed to provide you with practical steps to enhance your business development skills. Go through the workbook topics in the order presented since each theme builds on the one that precedes it. Some of the exercises will ask you to provide several examples (e.g. list 10 firm alumni). If you can only identify fewer than the requested number or examples, don't use that as an excuse to keep you from moving forward. You can always add more later.

Throughout the workbook, you will also find features called **TAKE 5** breaks. These breaks ask you to reflect on a particular topic, event, or business development experience. The results of each break will give you greater insight into the concepts being presented.

I've also created a series of short videos on www.youtube.com that provide explanations of the concepts in each chapter. To view this content, subscribe to takechargelegal on YouTube or access the following url: http://www.youtube.com/takechargelegal.

It's time to take charge of your legal career by learning how to develop business. Many have taken the path before you and have succeeded in building a sustaining and profitable book of business to support an enjoyable career. Turn the page and let's get started.

**Mary Carmel Kaczmarek, Esq.**
August 2013

*Chapter One introduces the concepts of marketing and business development and how they change at different thresholds in your career, much like the level and sophistication of your legal work changes as you gain experience. An exercise will help you identify your business development and practice style.*

- **Distinguishing Between Marketing and Business Development**
- **Business Development at Different Career Thresholds**
- **Business Development and Sustaining Practice Styles**

# CHAPTER ONE

# Starting *to* Take Charge

· · · · · · · ·

## Distinguishing Between Marketing *and* Business Development

Let's start by making certain you have a clear frame of reference as to what business development is all about, beginning by distinguishing it from marketing.

Marketing has its roots as a business discipline following World War II, when corporations' surplus capacity for manufacturing products met consumers' increased disposable income. Business owners sought to maximize that confluence by understanding or even creating consumer needs and wants. Over time, marketing concepts that were formerly applied only to products were expanded to include the marketing of services, including the services provided by lawyers and their firms.

Marketing is technically defined as a system of business practices that promote the mutually beneficial exchange of value between a buyer and a seller. The buyer or buyers are referred to as the "target market." A key concept related to marketing strategy is to determine the proper marketing mix, or combination of strategies for product, pricing, place and promotion—traditionally referred to as the "four Ps of marketing." Effective marketing strategy brings together the right combination of the four Ps of marketing. The theory is that when the mix of product (or services, in the case of law firms), pricing strategy, the place or location of the product or service delivery, and promotional efforts are properly calibrated to address the needs of a specific target market, then the mutually beneficial exchange of value is facilitated in a strategic and cost-effective way.

In most law firms, marketing activities—with one notable exception discussed below—are the focus of administrative professionals and firm leadership. It is their high-level task to determine organizational target markets, i.e., key industries or businesses that the firm is best positioned to target for business opportunities. They also identify key product or service offerings that connect well with the needs of defined target markets. Deciding on pricing strategies, whether to bill by the hour or to offer alternative fee arrangements, are also within the purview of management. The physical location for offices relative to the needs of the target market is also typically decided at the leadership level.

The one component of the marketing mix that is the responsibility of each lawyer in the firm is an aspect of promotion, which is person-to-person business development. Individual attorneys' focus on promotion strategy includes identifying and converting contacts into clients and then continuing to strengthen the relationship to cause the client to re-engage services when needed. The activity is also referred to as sales or business development. The focus of the *Practical Business Development Workbook* is to help you identify and implement the types of sales or promotional activities that are likely to bring in desirable new opportunities and promote client retention over time.

## Marketing Mix

Note the outer ring that surrounds the inner circle of the target market and the middle band of the four Ps. The elements in the outer ring are referred to as the five environmental factors—the economy, technological advances, competition, legal and political developments, and social and cultural changes. These environmental factors are in constant motion, and changes in any of them may impact the needs of the target market and the strategy for one or more of the four Ps. When developing a marketing plan and the related business development process, keep in mind how changes in any one of these areas may impact your sales approach to the target market.

For example, in 2012 Congress enacted the America Invents Act, a statute that caused significant changes to the way owners protect their innovations through federal patent law. Existing and potential clients need to be aware of the change in law and how it may impact their intellectual property holdings. So a promotional or business development tactic related to the change might be for an individual attorney to provide information and education to clients and prospects on the new law and its implications. Another environmental factor that you need to be aware of is the competition for your own and your firm's services. Knowing the unique competitive advantages that you or your firm have with respect to other legal service providers is key to distinguishing yourself with the target market. Do you see how changes in the environment may impact your marketing mix and approach to the target market?

## Business Development *at* Different Career Thresholds

Business development can and should be undertaken by an attorney throughout his or her career, beginning with the first year of practice. But just as a lawyer's substantive work changes over time, so should the level and degree of his or her business development efforts progress. Most attorneys initially engage in basic promotional and business development activities that they build on in intermediate and later stages of their careers.

Certain promotional and business development tasks should be accomplished in each of the three career "thresholds"—i.e., junior associate, more senior associate, and partner. Think of each of these thresholds as a developmental doorway that you must pass through to get to the next level of career success. There are no hard lines between the stages described below and you may overlap adjacent stages since your experience may exceed the typical time-related thresholds associated with each stage. Remember also that the activities in each stage create the foundation for those that follow later. The point is, if you haven't accomplished or addressed the activities of an earlier stage by the time you become a more senior associate, for example, you will have to "backfill" those building blocks before progressing to more advanced activities. Note, too, that a key to each career threshold is continuing to build on and advance in your substantive knowledge and practical legal skills. This is the value that you have to offer clients and without continually improving on your value proposition, you'll find that you don't have the necessary competitive advantage to obtain the best work from the best target clients.

**Junior Associate Career Threshold** *(Typically one to four years of practice)*

- Learn substantive skills and their practical application; become the best attorney you can
- Develop strong client service skills (responsiveness, preferences for information delivery and communication, listening, political savvy)
- Identify mentors and role models for substantive practice and client service
- Get educated about the firm's business
- Volunteer to work with more senior colleagues on their business development efforts
- Create and maintain a list of contacts, including classmates and new business contacts

**Midlevel to Senior Associate Threshold** *(Typically five to nine years of practice)*

- Hone a specific practice expertise that you enjoy and which creates the basis for a sustaining practice
- Know your clients and their businesses
- Build your profile by joining an association or a committee
- Continue to build your contact list
- Get involved in a professional organization and in business development networking
- Expand existing client relationships and begin to seek new business opportunities

**Partner Threshold** *(Typically ten or more years of practice)*

- Assume a leadership role in business development; show more junior colleagues the way
- Continue to build your reputation with relevant target markets
- Manage existing client relationships
- Actively seek new business opportunities
- Develop new service offerings and pricing strategies
- Continually add to substantive knowledge and practice skills

TAKE **5** : Career Threshold

Before proceeding, examine the activities related to your current career threshold. Assess whether you have or are now addressing the key promotional and business development activities of that stage. If not, identify what you will need to do to complete the activities to be prepared to move to the next threshold at the appropriate time.

# Business Development *and* Sustaining Practice Styles

Canadian attorney and legal consultant Timothy Leishman authored a fascinating article identifying what he describes as four sustaining practice styles. His premise is that depending on natural personality style and type of legal practice, attorneys tend to gravitate towards one of four categories of marketing and business development contribution to their firm's success. He refers to the four categories as "Sustaining Practice Styles," and he believes that to be successful, law firms need representatives of each category of business builder. His model is intended to replace the so-called "Finder, Minder, Grinder" model that was formerly used to describe the contributions of attorneys to a firm's practice.

Here are Leishman's four different categories of Sustaining Practice Styles and the key characteristics of each:

## The Rainmaker

- Business development strength: Networking
- Wins new business from new clients
- Externally focused
- Emphasis on building relationships (e.g., networks, entertains, sits on boards, involved in community causes)
- Referred to as a firm ambassador

## The Hired Gun

- Business development strength: Building reputation
- Wins new business from new clients
- Externally focused
- Emphasis on showcasing expertise (e.g., writes/publishes articles, white papers; speaks at conferences)
- Known as someone who enhances firm's reputation

### The Brain Surgeon

- Business development strength: Research and development
- Wins new business from existing clients
- Internally focused
- Emphasis on expertise (e.g., develops new strategies, products; creates competitive advantage for firm in specialty areas)
- Known as an innovator or someone who really is smarter than everyone else in the firm

### Point Person

- Business development strength: Client service
- Wins new business from existing clients
- Internally focused
- Emphasis on relationships (e.g., gets to know clients, multiple contacts at each; creates client development events and opportunities)
- Known for managing major client accounts and cementing long-term relationships

---

## EXERCISE | Your Sustaining Practice Style

Study the model—based on Leishman's research—and identify your practice style and related business development strengths. This reflection may be useful to you in adapting the basic principles of business development to a style that is natural and comfortable to you.

I am most like a ___Point Person___, because my natural strengths for building and expanding business include: ___developing ongoing + new business with___ ___Clients like IMGICLC + Energizer___

Which of the sustaining practice styles is typical of the most successful attorneys in your practice area? How does your typical style match up?

___Rainmaker - Charlie/Bill___
___Brain Surgeon - Ted/Jerre___

*Business development follows a two-part cycle where the first part of the cycle deals with identifying prospective clients and making an initial sale of legal services to them. The second half of the cycle relates to building a relationship with the client throughout the process of providing legal services. Chapter Two helps you understand the cycle and what you need to focus on to be a successful business developer.*

- **Part One of the Business Development Cycle: Targeting New Opportunities**
- **Part Two of the Business Development Cycle: Expanding Current Relationships**

CHAPTER TWO

# Understanding *the* Business Development Cycle

• • • • • • • •

Valerie A. Zeithaml, a professor of services marketing at The University of North Carolina aptly describes the proper focus for professional services firms' marketing efforts: "Under the old marketing concept, the objective was to make a sale. Under the new marketing concept, the objective is to develop a relationship, in which the sale is only the beginning. The client is a long-term strategic asset." Zeithaml's observation illustrates the two aspects of what is known as the business development cycle. If you accept the concept presented in Chapter One—i.e., that the promotional activity of developing business with specific contacts who are prospects and clients of your practice is your responsibility—then you must understand and appreciate the specific tasks associated with both stages of the process.

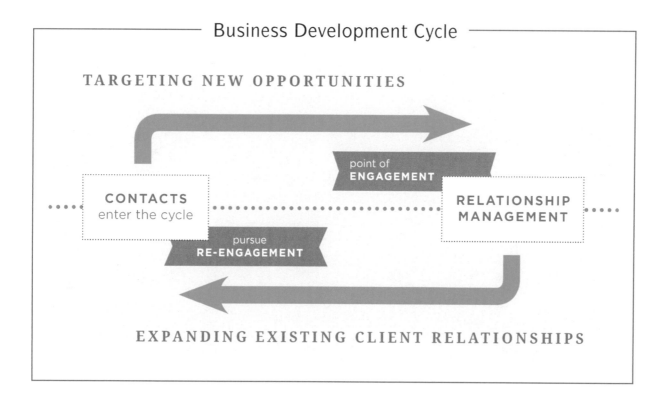

The first aspect deals with identifying prospective clients and making an initial sale of legal services to them. The second half of the cycle relates to building a relationship with the client throughout the process of providing legal services. The goal is to maximize the asset of the relationship by taking steps that will predispose the client to re-engage you and the firm in future matters. Successful business developers are proactive in targeting new opportunities and managing them to the point of engagement or initial sale. They also invest in nurturing the client relationship throughout the course of a project or case, developing the strategic asset that each client represents.

Before describing the specific strategies used to target new opportunities and manage relationships to the point of sale, it will help to understand the key steps of each aspect of the business development cycle.

# Part One *of the* Business Development Cycle: Targeting New Opportunities

Your firm has an existing base of clients at this point. But somewhere along the line, historically, those were prospective opportunities. Through what process did they become clients? The firm founders are probably not available to explain to you how this worked in the past, but initially, through the founding attorneys' proactive efforts, prospective client contacts entered into the new business development cycle. Those original entrepreneurs "pulled" those contacts into the business development cycle probably by first determining if there was a need for the firm's services. This process is generally referred to as "qualifying prospects" for business development.

Whether either party of the qualification process was aware of it or not, in a casual conversation on the golf course, over lunch, or at a professional organization meeting, the "lawyer-seller" was asking some general questions about the potential needs of the "client-buyer" for legal services. The attorney's inquires may have included questions such as:

- What are your company's current priorities?
- What kind of opportunities are there for your business right now?
- Have you heard about the pending legislation? Do you have any thoughts on what kind of impact it may have on your business unit?
- Tell me about the company's legal resources. What kind of cases or projects do they typically help you with?
- What business needs or concerns keep you up at night?

The responses to these discussion points indicate to the attorney how likely it is that the potential buyer has a proximate need for his or her services. In a nutshell, this is how the qualification of prospects works. If the would-be-seller develops a sense that there may be a real need for his or her legal services, then a decision is made to initiate the formal process of business development.

What does it mean to initiate the process of business development? A good analogy is the dating and courtship ritual that romantic couples pursue. At first, there is a "getting to know you" phase that requires a number of meaningful points of contact. For legal business development, this may include attending professional networking events or community activities with the prospect, sharing articles of interest, visiting the prospect at his or her business location, and entertaining at social or sporting events. It is through these encounters that the prospect develops a sense of your capabilities and what it might be like to work with you on a legal matter. At the same time, you are developing a sense of whether this individual and her company is indeed an excellent client prospect.

Whether a contact is an "excellent client prospect" depends on a variety of factors. Here's a short list of what may go into that consideration:

- Are the legal issues that may be involved in representing the prospect within the firm's or your own core strengths?
- Do you like this person? Would this be a potentially positive client relationship based on what you know about this individual?
- Does the prospect have the financial resources to pay for the firm's services?
- Would representing this prospective client create an ethical or business conflict for the firm?
- Is this a one-time project or is there potential for continued legal services?

As you engage in the getting-to-know-you process—usually over the course of several conversations and email exchanges of a few months' time—you reach the point at which it either makes sense to disengage the business development process (because you've concluded that this would not make a good client opportunity) or you decide to advance the relationship to the point of asking for business. The more experience you have with this part of the business development process, the more developed your judgment will become regarding these decisions. When you initially become active in targeting new opportunities, you want to ask for advice from a mentor with more experience in the business development process. He or she may provide very helpful guidance and help you to invest time wisely in this important business activity.

It may be worthwhile to consider a hypothetical associate's experience in developing business. Cathy recently met Tamika, in-house counsel at Acme Company, at a community fund-raising event. Standing together talking in the drink line they discovered that they were both graduates of the same law school and prior to going in-house at Acme, Tamika had been in private practice similar to Cathy's. Tamika is new to town and to Acme, and she wants to get to know more people in the local business community. Having studied the *Practical Workbook*, Cathy senses that Tamika may be an excellent prospect for her business development efforts. Before parting company at the fund-raising event, she asks Tamika for her card and indicates that she will be following up soon to talk more about their similar backgrounds and figure out how she may introduce Tamika to other business contacts.

Within a day or so of attending the event, Cathy connects to Tamika on the social networking site, LinkedIn. She learns more about Tamika's experience to date by studying her profile and that of Acme Company. She sees that Acme may be a good client opportunity for the firm, and decides to invest time getting to know Tamika better, not only to help her to get settled in the business community, but to also explore the potential—at some point—to do work with her. Over a period of several months, Cathy forms an enjoyable business friendship with Tamika. Starting with a lunch meeting to become better acquainted with her, Cathy learns that Tamika would like to join the board of a local non-profit, and helps her—with assistance from Cathy's firm colleagues—to identify one that is a good fit. In time she learns from Tamika that Acme presently has a nearly exclusive relationship with the Smith Jones law firm, which does most of the company's outside legal work. Cathy also discovers that the Smith Jones law firm lacks certain specialty practices—such as intellectual property capabilities—that Acme needs. Patiently and systematically, Cathy advances her relationship with Tamika to the point where Tamika—recognizing the gap in Smith Jones' capabilities—offers to introduce Cathy to Acme's general counsel to talk about the IP services that Cathy's firm has to offer. Within 12 months of commencing her new business development efforts with Tamika, Cathy brings in Acme as a new client.

## Part Two *of the* Business Development Cycle: Expanding Current Relationships

Once a prospect—like our example of Tamika and Acme—makes the decision to engage your legal services, you embark on the second phase in the business development cycle. Only true business development naturals appreciate that, at the point of engagement by the prospect, not only are they serving a specific need for legal services, but they are also seeking to develop a relationship that will go beyond the initial project. Business development naturals, and those who have become adept through practice, appreciate Professor Zeithaml's insight that "the client is a long-term strategic asset." After investing significant time advancing the relationship to the point of engagement, it would be shortsighted to focus only on doing the work and to miss the opportunity to develop a relationship that leads to ongoing opportunities.

What does it mean to manage a client relationship as part of an overall business development strategy? It means investing non-billable time to develop and nurture the relationship while you are on the assignment. Start the process by establishing the client's expectations for service. With Acme, you want to spend time "off the meter" (i.e., non-billable time), asking for information about the client contact's service expectations.  Find out, for example:

- Would you like a written or verbal report of our progress on the matter?
- What's the best way to reach you if we have a problem?
- Who besides you may be interested in progress reports?  Will you forward that information or would you like us to include others in the company in the process?
- How involved would you and your team like to be in developing the strategy for the project?
- What is our budget for the project?
- What would be a successful outcome on this project?
- What are your pet peeves when it comes to working with outside counsel?
- What are best practices for service that you would like us to integrate into our work?

At the same time that you take time to learn about the client's expectations, let her know you will be checking in from time to time to be sure your own and the firm's work is meeting expectations. You want to be able to make a mid-course correction if indicated. Say you'll do it, and then be sure to follow through and make any necessary adjustments in your own performance or that of others on the team.

Think about it: All together, this type of initial interview will take less than an hour of your time, depending on the sophistication and complexity of the matter. But it has the potential to make a tremendous difference in how the client perceives you and the firm and your ability to meet and exceed expectations on the first project. It's a great investment in taking charge of your career and building business now and into the future.

Other investment strategies for managing client relationships well and effectively include:

- Thanking the client for the opportunity to do business with her. It may sound like a small matter, but it's important to acknowledge that the client has trusted you with her work and you appreciate it.
- Tracking the client and its key players in the news using any number of Internet-based services.
- Conducting a feedback session at the conclusion of the project. Ask specifically what the client liked particularly about your performance and what you might have done differently to better serve the client's needs. This applies to relationships at all levels, i.e., whether a partner talking with the general counsel or an associate sharing with a counterpart in the client organization. Ask the person you worked closest with if they have any tips on how to improve the way you provide a service or if there was anything she thought you did particularly well.
- Inviting the client to relevant firm events or other educational meetings that you believe she would enjoy or appreciate. Attend with her and introduce her to colleagues as appropriate.
- Offering to present a program at the client's offices on a legal topic of interest, or to provide an update to the client team on the status of the case or project.
- If it is an authentic compliment, then praising the client and her team for their efforts and involvement in the case or project. If your client contact is junior in her organization, consider whether it would be appropriate to mention exemplary performance to her supervisor.

There are many more things you can do to invest in a client relationship while managing the billable project. Such investments typically pay great dividends in terms of repeat business and new opportunities.

# TAKE 5: Ask an Attorney

Identify two senior attorneys in your firm who get good results at business development. Schedule a short conversation with each to ask a few questions about strategies they use in both parts of the business development cycle.

**Consider asking:**

- Share with me how you brought in your first significant client. What steps did you take to develop that opportunity?
- Describe a time when you were instrumental in expanding a relationship with an existing client of the firm. What was particularly effective in building the relationship?
- What do you know now about business development that you wish you had known earlier in your career?
- What advice do you have for me about getting involved in business development?

Take note of each person's responses and consider how their advice tracks with the ideas in this chapter, keeping in mind the science (i.e., discipline and process) and art (i.e., personal approach) of business development. Which of your contacts' comments related to the science of business development? Which had to do more with personal style or the art of business development? What did you learn that you may wish to incorporate into your own approach to building business?

*The market for legal services is infinite. To be successful, you need to narrow your focus on a targeted market to be efficient and effective as a business developer. Chapter Three will help you define your target market.*

- Identifying Model Clients in the Target Market
- Understanding the Target Market's Needs for Legal Services
- Target Clients Include Other Attorneys in Your Firm
- Review the "Marketing Mix" Regularly to Maintain Your Focus on the Target Market

CHAPTER THREE

# Identifying Target Clients *and* Their Needs *for* Legal Services

· · · · · · ·

## Identifying Model Clients *in the* Target Market

Chapter One distinguished between the business discipline of marketing and the practice of business development. You will recall that marketing was described as a high-level determination of the key target markets, pricing strategy, location or place of business, and promotional activities. It was also pointed out that the broad overview of the marketing process is usually the responsibility of firm leadership. The marketing mix diagram is also a useful starting point for an individual attorney to identify his or her target clients—and specific members of that target market—and to develop an overall strategy for successful person-to-person business development.

| EXERCISE | Ideal Target Market |
|----------|---------------------|

Successful business development by an individual lawyer requires that he or she identify in general terms the ideal target market for his or her services. This is typically going to be a business in a particular industry (e.g., health care, real estate, manufacturing) or a particular type of business (e.g., a public company, an employer of more than 100 people, a family-owned business) with a specific type of legal need (e.g., litigation, transactional work, advice and counsel).

For example, a product liability litigator would have as a target market "companies that make things which injure people fairly regularly such as car and appliance manufacturers."

You see how this works:  You make a connection between what you do substantively and the target type of client that typically uses your services.

It is useful to identify your specific target market by doing a forensic analysis of your "ideal clients" historically. In the space provided, jot down specific past or current clients who you consider to be model targets for your particular practice. Next to each client name, indicate the reasons you consider each to be an ideal client for your practice.

Your reasons may include factors such as, *"this was a sophisticated client in a merger and acquisition project that gave me the opportunity to challenge my legal skills and to stretch,"* or *"this was a particularly profitable litigation case for me and my practice group and it was great not to be scrutinized for each time entry and expense."*

| "IDEAL" CLIENTS TO DATE | REASONS |
|-------------------------|---------|
| 1 | |
| 2 | |
| 3 | |
| 4 | |
| 5 | |

# Understanding *the* Target Market's Needs *for* Legal Services— Now *and in the* Future

By doing some historical analysis of your ideal client relationships, you can figure out the legal services or "products" (in marketing speak) that are most in demand by your specific target market. It's important to do some research by reviewing time records for a period of 12 to 24 months to confirm your recollection of what types of legal services were in highest demand. The review will help you identify the current legal needs of the clients you wish to work with. This then is what you have to sell to your primary targets.

Keep in mind that your services or the "product" you offer consist not only of what you do, but how you do it. While most non-lawyer clients don't appreciate the substantive nuances of legal work product, they have strong opinions about the way in which legal services are provided. An important aspect of the product or legal service you provide to clients includes factors such as responsiveness, timeliness, user-friendliness and cost-effectiveness. As you further develop your understanding of how to bring in new and desirable business for your firm, don't discount the competitive significance of the way in which you provide services.

Analyzing the target market's need for legal services also requires you to think prospectively. You know what clients need and want now from you and your firm, but highly successful business developers try to gauge the future needs and wants of the target market as well in light of developments in the business environment. They consider, for example, how technology may be better used to serve the needs of the target market. They focus on pending legislation and case law developments that might impact a client's need for legal services and advice. The focus is on being "first to market" in anticipating key client concerns and as a result, promoting a solution ahead of the competition.

TAKE 5: Think Prospectively

Think about the case law or relevant regulations that are developing in your area of practice right now. Which of those has the potential to have a major impact on a target client's business or industry? What steps can you start to take now to educate the client regarding the ramifications of those developments and to offer new services to address those needs?

## Target Clients Include Other Attorneys *in* Your Firm

Depending on your career threshold as described in Chapter One, a good bit of your substantive work may come to you from other attorneys in your firm. In the same way that you analyze model external clients, you also want to identify which attorneys in the firm to target for more business opportunities. For example, a senior associate with a niche practice of technology licensing would want to target corporate practice attorneys whose clients license technology as part of their business operations. In this illustration, the corporate partner is a referral source for the licensing attorney, and could be an excellent source of new business opportunities if the licensing professional develops an influential relationship with him. If you think about it, a very efficient way to build a sustaining practice is to position yourself as a "go-to" expert in a particular area of law that may be in demand by many clients of your firm. In Timothy Leishman's analysis of Sustaining Practice Styles, this would be the type of approach used by The Brain Surgeon. Be sure to include in your target market analysis a review of those firm colleagues who have referred work to you in the past that fits into the target category.

## Review *the* "Marketing Mix" Regularly
## *to* Maintain Your Focus *on the* Target Market

Most associates do not have primary responsibility for developing the pricing of legal services or determining the physical place in which those services will be provided and an in-depth discussion of those issues is beyond the scope of the *Practical Workbook*. It does make sense, though, for you to review the firm's strategic plan and your practice group's business growth plan to make sure your personal efforts are being guided by the higher level vision for those aspects of the marketing mix. In addition, keep an eye on changes in the so-called environmental factors described in Chapter One.

## TAKE 5: Impact of Environment Change on Your Service Offerings

Consider how a demographic shift currently underway in our American society impacts a key target market and a service offering of many general practice firms. The issue is the aging of the baby-boomer generation. As the largest segment of the American population approaches retirement age, its needs for different types of legal services and advice is also changing. The successful vice president of a corporation who is also a baby-boomer will need assistance for estate planning and potentially for changes to his corporation's compensation structure. As baby-boomers age, health-care providers must consider changes in legislation that will impact Medicare and Medicaid funding requirements and the obligations of providers. Because baby-boomers represent such a large percentage of the voting population, their needs and wants will have a great impact on politics and potential legal changes.

Pay attention to the environmental factors that impact your key target markets. Depending on your particular focus and legal service area, at any given time one or more of the environmental factors may require a change in the service you offer, the way in which you offer it, the price you sell it for and the way you promote yourself to the target market.

*Business development starts with your efforts to identify and build prospective client relationships. Your firm may target businesses, but your targets are individuals. Chapter Four will help you identify your very best prospects and manage your outreach to those key contacts.*

- **A Critical Task for Building Business: Developing a Personal List of Target Market Contacts**
- **Building Your 10X10 Matrix**
- **The Next Step: Using the 10X10 Matrix to Create Your Best Opportunities List**

CHAPTER FOUR

# Key Strategies *for* Creating *a* List *of* Target Market Contacts *and* Mining It

• • • • • • • •

## A Critical Task *for* Building Business: Developing a Personal List *of* Target Market Contacts

The goal of business development is to add new clients to your practice and to expand existing client relationships. Early on in the process you will have to move beyond generalities of the activity and develop a personal list of target contacts. As discussed in Chapter Two, you need a list of prospective client contacts that have been qualified as potential clients for your practice as well as a list of existing client contacts with whom to expand relationships and business opportunities.

Individual attorneys typically build business with and through their individual contacts. The firm's strategy may be—and in most cases should be—to target corporations or other types of business entities for business development purposes. But people develop new work through their relationships with other people. In this chapter, you will be asked to think about your contacts in 10 categories of relationships. By analyzing your current universe of contacts, you will learn how to create a prioritized list of what is called "best opportunities for new business." You will see how to create a "B List" of all your other contacts. Both are valuable and should be tended and nurtured. But the high priority or "Best Opportunities List" of individuals requires a more meaningful investment of time and attention to advance each relationship to the point of engagement as an actual client of the firm.

Attorneys with limited business development experience tend to have a fear response to the idea of creating a contact list of opportunities for business. Some common reactions are "but I don't know anyone who could be a potential client of my practice" or "I am sort of an introvert and I haven't stayed in touch with classmates and former colleagues who might be the source of business." A good way to manage this anxiety is to move forward with the process of researching and developing a contact list as suggested below. As you begin on the necessary research and the process, you may find that even if your current contacts are not an immediate source of business opportunities for you, many of them are connected to a separate universe of contacts that does include the type of people who can send business your way. It is just a matter of suspending your disbelief at this point and getting started on the 10X10 Matrix exercise.

**Converting contacts into clients is a numbers game.**

**5-10 exposures** before a qualified prospect or target makes a buying decision.

**3 out of 10 targets** will be converted to actual new clients (and that's if you have been diligent in your pursuit). Just as in baseball, a .300 average is an excellent outcome for new business development purposes.

**18 months** is the average time it takes to land a client from start to finish, and it may take as long as several years.

**30 minutes** each day spent on business development on average is the personal goal you need to set. Converting clients to contacts requires commitment. *The Practical Workbook* provides plenty of practical activities to help you meet your commitment to invest time in building new business opportunities. The sooner you get going in a strategic and disciplined way, the sooner you'll see meaningful results.

# Building Your 10x10 Matrix

You get to the "Best Opportunities for New Business List" by first building a matrix describing the universe of your current business contacts. This is known as the 10x10 Matrix. Completing the matrix begins as a brainstorming exercise. An important aspect of brainstorming is to remind yourself not to make judgments as you go—just let the ideas flow. The editing comes later.

There are 10 groups of existing contacts that you will need to examine to build the 10x10 matrix. Your Outlook and LinkedIn contacts, holiday card list, smartphone call log, billing timesheets, and whatever other tool you use to communicate with and track your key contacts in all facets of your business life will become the best resources to use to refresh your recollection and begin building your matrix. A good rule of thumb is to include in your matrix only people who will recognize your name in a positive way if you get in touch with them at this point. So you may want to leave off contacts with whom your relationship has truly gone cold for more than 10 years.

The 10x10 Matrix worksheet provides space for 10 contacts in each category. Your objective is to fill in as many names as possible, with no fewer than 25 and no more than 100 contacts in the entire matrix. Here are the categories of contacts that you should consider:

*Former clients:* Sometimes it is difficult to know when a client is a "former" client so consider client contacts you have not worked with in the last two to four years. You are looking for individuals who are familiar with your legal skills. Remember to include in the category of "former clients" individuals who no longer exist in the capacity in which you provided the legal service, such as the seller of a business or individuals who left the client as part of the legal service you provided (an example would be in a merger).

*Referral sources:* Include other professional service providers such as financial advisers, accountants, business brokers, and lawyers from other law firms.

*Former colleagues:* This category consists of undergraduate and law school classmates, fellow summer associates who joined other law firms, people you may have clerked with, and co-workers from jobs you had prior to joining a law firm.

*Firm alumni:* Unless someone left on truly bad terms and his/her professionalism is in question, consider him/her a potential contact regardless of where he/she is now employed.

*Experts and consultants:* This group consists of professionals you've worked with in the course of handling matters or cases for clients, or who you've met in business or professional development activities.

*Opposing counsel:* These are the attorneys who sat at the other table—in the courtroom or the conference room. If you developed mutual respect for each other over the course of a case or transaction, you may wish to include such counsel on your matrix. This is the group when asked if they had to hire an attorney, you would want them to drop your name.

*Community organizations:* Pull out the membership and committee lists of the community organizations where you hold a position or support the work, and identify individuals as potential clients or referral sources.

*Professional organizations:* These will most likely be other attorneys you have worked with through your local or specialty bar association or the American Bar Association, but also those individuals you have met through other industry-focused associations, such as Turnaround Management Association, National Association of Women Lawyers, National Association of Health Care Lawyers, etc.

*Personal friends and contacts:* Consider individuals with whom you have crossed paths through your children's school activities, your family, your book club, your health club, your golf league, and other friends. If you've had business-related conversations with anyone in these groups, they may be a potential source of new opportunity for you.

*Other:* Who did you miss that may not fit neatly into a category?

**Using the chart below, construct the 10x10 Matrix for yourself.** *Use the current universe of your "warm" contacts for business development. It will be an important tool in your business development efforts and it is required for the next steps in the business-building process.*

### FORMER CLIENTS (PAST 3 YEARS)

| 1 | |
|---|---|
| 2 | |
| 3 | |
| 4 | |
| 5 | |
| 6 | |
| 7 | |
| 8 | |
| 9 | |
| 10 | |

### REFERRAL SOURCES

| 1 | |
|---|---|
| 2 | |
| 3 | |
| 4 | |
| 5 | |
| 6 | |
| 7 | |
| 8 | |
| 9 | |
| 10 | |

## COLLEAGUES / FORMER COLLEAGUES

1
2
3
4
5
6
7
8
9
10

## FIRM ALUMNI

1
2
3
4
5
6
7
8
9
10

## EXPERTS / CONSULTANTS

| | |
|---|---|
| 1 | |
| 2 | |
| 3 | |
| 4 | |
| 5 | |
| 6 | |
| 7 | |
| 8 | |
| 9 | |
| 10 | |

## OPPOSING COUNSEL

| | |
|---|---|
| 1 | |
| 2 | |
| 3 | |
| 4 | |
| 5 | |
| 6 | |
| 7 | |
| 8 | |
| 9 | |
| 10 | |

## CIVIC / COMMUNITY GROUPS

1
2
3
4
5
6
7
8
9
10

## PROFESSIONAL ORGANIZATIONS / SOCIAL MEDIA

1
2
3
4
5
6
7
8
9
10

| EXERCISE | Build Your Matrix |
|---|---|

## PERSONAL FRIENDS / FAMILY

1
2
3
4
5
6
7
8
9
10

## OTHER

1
2
3
4
5
6
7
8
9
10

# The Next Step: Using *the* 10x10 Matrix *to* Create Your Best Opportunities *for* New Business List

So now you have identified the entire universe—as it exists right now—of a strong cross-section of your current contacts in 10 different categories. They are what you might call "warm contacts," i.e., people who to the best of your knowledge will recognize your name with little prompting because you now have or in the past had a positive relationship with each of them. Perhaps your list has 25 entries or as many as 100. Regardless of the number, your task now is to promote 15 contacts out of this total universe to "The Best Opportunities for New Business List."

As a general concept, it is difficult for a busy professional who has billable hour and other important obligations to spend much more than an average of five hours each week on business development. Recognizing that business development includes not only person-to-person sales efforts but also other strategic activities, the focal point for your individual efforts should be a list of no more than 15 best opportunities. The balance of the contacts you identified in the 10x10 Matrix will be the focus of less intensive cultivation efforts and more likely "low-touch" or "no-touch" tactics (e.g., general distribution of news releases, invitations to firm events, updates on legal developments, and invitations to connect on LinkedIn). The list of remaining contacts on the 10x10 Matrix may be considered to be your "B List" of prospective client opportunities.

So what is the methodology for deciding which contacts to promote from the 10x10 Matrix to the Best Opportunities List of 15? To begin the process, you will need to sort through all of the contacts on your 10x10 Matrix and make judgment calls as you go. With respect to each contact listed, ask yourself, "Is this individual a 'best opportunity'?  Why or why not?" If you are like most attorneys, some of your contacts will readily rise to the top (i.e., it will be apparent that they belong on the Best Opportunities List), while others will clearly belong on the B List. In close cases when it's not clear on which list a contact belongs, consider the following "best practices" for promotion:

- If you can easily identify a specific new business opportunity with a particular contact, then he/she should probably be promoted to the Best Opportunities List. For example, if Antonio Peters, an alumnus of the firm, is now assistant general counsel at Lincoln Corporation, and he has indicated the potential for you to do business with his new organization at the appropriate time, then Antonio belongs on the Best Opportunities List. He presents an actual and definable opportunity for new business (i.e., a chance to work with him and his new employer when the time is right). On the other hand, another hypothetical former firm attorney, Cary Sims, is now corporate counsel at Miramar Partners. While you exchange friendly email messages from time to time, you have never gotten a signal from Cary that he is inclined to send work to you and the firm. Cary is a contact you will want to try to cultivate, but at this point he does not represent the same type of "best opportunity" that Antonio does.

- Depending on the nature of your practice, you may want to promote only local area contacts to your Best Opportunities List. For example, if yours is a real estate or estate planning practice located in Pennsylvania, it is unlikely that your Uncle Bob in Florida—despite his many business connections and potential for Florida-based referrals—will be able to connect you with opportunities that you may capitalize on. If, on the other hand, yours is a federal or national type of practice (e.g., intellectual property or public company representation in corporate governance issues), then Uncle Bob may have great potential for referrals and opportunities and he should make the cut for Best Opportunities List.

- If you have less than 15 contacts that it makes sense to promote to the Best Opportunities List, then work with what you have. It's important to focus your personal efforts only on contacts that have potential to lead to new business. If you spend your time trying to cultivate contacts that don't present real opportunities, it's unlikely that you'll obtain worthwhile results and, worse than that, you may start thinking that it's a waste of time to work at building your business. That's only true if and when you focus on unpromising contacts.

Are you starting to see how this prioritization process works?

## TAKE 5: Best Opportunities List Sample

Look over the Sample Best Opportunties List below. Note that the WHO, WHERE, WHAT and WHY columns have been completed with hypothetical information for each promoted or Best Opportunities contact. Consider this information as you review the instructions for completing your own Best Opportunities List.

| WHO (Prospect Name) | WHERE (Organization) | WHAT (Describe Opportunities) | WHY (Potential Value / Likelihood of Success) | HOW/WHEN (Strategies / Dates; List at least three) |
|---|---|---|---|---|
| 1  **Len Smith** Former client | Now IP counsel at Acme Corp | Opportunities to work with new organization  Positive reference  Referrals to former colleagues at Beta | High Value /  Medium likelihood of success | |
| 2  **Sally Dean** Fellow board member with American Red Cross | Attorney with Jones & Jones | Can do local counsel work for her  Her firm has no M&A attorneys | Medium Value /  High likelihood of success | |
| 3  **Kelly Hope** Law school alum | Assistant GC at International Housewares | Opportunities to do M&A deals | Medium Value /  Medium likelihood of success | |

Key pieces of data that will help you determine the business development priority to be given to a particular contact relate to the two variables described in the "WHY" column of the Best Opportunities List. The category requires you to answer two questions. The first is "**What is the potential value** of the work that may come from this opportunity?" Use the rankings "High," "Medium" or "Low" to rate the potential value that the work and the relationship may have for your practice. This will be a guesstimate in most cases, but for now suspend your disbelief and use your best judgment in rating the potential value of the work and the relationship. Be sure to rate the potential value relative to your own practice right now rather than the firm's overall practice; you may not have contacts now that will create significant business opportunities for the firm as a whole, but they may be very meaningful and valuable for your personal work at this time.

The second question posed by the WHY column variables (again, based on what you currently know) is **"What is the likelihood that I will succeed** in obtaining new business from this contact if I am systematic and diligent in my business development efforts?" Use the same rankings of High, Medium or Low to rate your likelihood of success in obtaining business from this contact *based on what you know now about the opportunity*, again making a notation in the column on the Best Opportunities worksheet. If you have no basis upon which to make even a guesstimate of likelihood of success based on your knowledge of and relationship to the contact, then he/she probably does not belong on this high priority contact list.

Do you see how the two variables in the WHY column will help you to prioritize your business development efforts? For example, whenever an opportunity has a High/High designation (indicating high potential value for your practice and a high likelihood that you may succeed in bringing in the business), that should be the first focus of your strategic business-building activities. On the other hand, when you see a linkage of the variables Low/Low in the WHY column for a particular contact, then you may wish to practice your business-building efforts on that contact, but not make it a first priority for your time and best efforts.

If you find yourself in the fortunate position of having more than 15 contacts who you believe should be promoted to the Business Opportunities List, then make a judgment call considering other variables for inclusion or exclusion. For example, if two of your contacts appear to be excellent opportunities both with high value and high likelihood of success for potential business development, then base your decisions on the last time you were in direct personal contact with each individual or your personal chemistry with him or her. Your efforts are more likely to be successful if you enjoy your interactions with the individual. (See "Ranking Your Relationships" in Chapter Six for another perspective on ranking clients.)

If you've gotten to this point in the *Practical Workbook* and have completed your B List and your Best Opportunities List—congratulations! You have reached a significant milestone on the path to taking control of your career by learning to build business. In Chapter Five, you'll see how to complete the HOW column on the Best Opportunities List and you'll be well on your way to creating new business for yourself and your firm.

## TAKE 5: Firm Resources

Speak with the professional staff members in the firm's marketing or business development department to learn about the type of database capabilities the firm has for CRM (Contact Relationship Management) or ERM (Enterprise Relationship Management) and how you can use the database to track your contacts and for cultivating your Best Opportunities List.

It may also help to sit down with firm marketing and business development professionals and possibly your firm's research team to learn about the type of support they may provide to help you learn more about the contacts on your Best Opportunities List. The research may provide important information for further developing the relationships.

So now you have identified the contacts you wish to promote to the Best Opportunities List.

The name of the contact goes in the WHO column, and the organization he/she is associated with should be inserted in the WHERE column.

In the WHAT column, you must describe as specifically as possible the opportunity that the contact represents for new business development.

In the WHY column, proceed to rank each contact, using the variables "High," "Medium," and "Low" to describe the potential value each opportunity represents, as well as the likelihood you will succeed in getting the business if you are strategic and systematic in **HOW** you proceed to develop it.

| WHO (Prospect Name) | WHERE (Organization) | WHAT (Describe Opportunities) | WHY (Potential Value / Likelihood of Success) | HOW/WHEN (Strategies / Dates; List at least three) |
|---|---|---|---|---|
| 1 | | | | |
| 2 | | | | |
| 3 | | | | |
| 4 | | | | |
| 5 | | | | |
| 6 | | | | |

| WHO (Prospect Name) | WHERE (Organization) | WHAT (Describe Opportunities) | WHY (Potential Value / Likelihood of Success) | HOW/WHEN (Strategies / Dates; List at least three) |
|---|---|---|---|---|
| 7 | | | | |
| 8 | | | | |
| 9 | | | | |
| 10 | | | | |
| 11 | | | | |
| 12 | | | | |
| 13 | | | | |
| 14 | | | | |
| 15 | | | | |

*Chapter Five takes you through the steps of converting the best opportunities as you have identified them into clients. It is a methodical process and one that will help improve your conversion rate.*

- **#1: Research and Plan (and Repeat)**
- **#2: Set Realistic Goals for Advancing Relationships with Each Contact**
- **#3: Ask for the Business**
- **#4: Ask at the Right Time**
- **#5: Ask the Right Person**

CHAPTER FIVE

# Five Best Practices *for* Converting Contacts *into* Clients

• • • • • • • •

Now that you have invested time and effort creating your Best Opportunities List, it's time to maximize the return on investment by developing customized strategies to advance your relationship with each contact to the point of engagement. This chapter focuses on the five best practices for converting contacts into clients. Using the Best Opportunities List, you'll learn how to craft customized approaches to each of your targets and to follow through to convert 30 percent of those targets to new work.

The application of these practices will help you to populate the HOW column in the Best Opportunities List. While the strategies described below won't provide you with specific tactics to implement for each of your priority contacts, they should prompt you to develop customized approaches to advance the relationship with each of your Best Opportunities to the point where it is appropriate to ask for the business.

## #1: Research and Plan (and Repeat)

Think of each contact on your Best Opportunities List as a potential client or source of new business opportunities. Your ultimate goal is to pursue a plan of action that results in a client engagement through your cultivation of each contact. You need to develop a "mini plan" or customized process for advancing the relationship for each of your key contacts. In some cases, this may be a time-consuming activity and that's why in Chapter Four you were encouraged to focus your attention primarily on a short list of 15 "Best Opportunities" versus scattering your attention across lower-ranking opportunities.

Every attorney is aware that research or due diligence is necessary to develop an accurate understanding of a particular legal situation or problem. In the same way, research is needed to determine whether a contact on your Best Opportunities List is in fact a contact that could be developed into a client relationship or is otherwise a source of business referrals. Personal interactions provide the primary research to help you determine if a particular contact has a need for your services and whether you and your firm would be a good fit for the client's work.

Let's say that you meet Sasha at a professional conference. Sasha is assistant general counsel at her company and responsible for employment-related litigation, which happens to be your practice focus as well. You have a lively conversation with her at one of the lunch breaks and she describes to you how as a result of a recent merger with another company that did not have the same sophisticated human resources policies as her legacy company, she is concerned about significant potential litigation. Based on your conversation with Sasha and the rapport you quickly established with each other, you decide that she may be an excellent addition to your Best Opportunities List. Now your challenge is how to develop the relationship to the point where it would be appropriate to ask for the opportunity to be of service to her and her company, recognizing that she most likely is already working with another firm which you will have to displace at least to some extent. This is where the initial research comes in—first primary research gathered through connecting with her in building the relationship, and then secondary research culled through publicly available information about her and her company.

Keep in mind that occasionally you will meet a contact who will have an immediate need for your services. In other words, every once in a while, business developers find themselves in just the right spot when "lightning strikes." Most of the time, however, it takes time to advance the relationship with the contact to the point where it is appropriate to talk about doing business together. Developing a plan based on your interactions with a contact like Sasha and your secondary research is the best way to ensure that you will stimulate a "lightning strike" that allows you to create a new client relationship.

In Chapter Four, you developed a Best Opportunities List. So far, you have completed all the columns of information except for the "HOW" column, which relates to devising strategies for developing the contact relationship and opportunity. Before going any further in Chapter Five, focus on the first three contacts that you list in the "WHO" column of your Best Opportunities List and describe the secondary and primary research you should do now to understand how to best pursue each opportunity.

Using the example of Sasha, you may decide it would be worthwhile to conduct a search of the complaints filed against her legacy company so you get an idea of who your competition may be for the employment litigation that Sasha outsources. In addition, you will want to connect with Sasha as soon as possible following the conference before Sasha forgets the pleasant conversation you had and learn more about her situation (this is your primary research at this point) to position yourself as a potentially helpful resource for her.

As you work on your research strategy, you will need to develop specific questions to ask each of your contacts to learn more about his/her situation and to begin to better understand whether this is in fact a "best opportunity" for you. Don't ask questions that can be answered easily with a bit of secondary research (e.g., "Where are your plants located?"). Review the following questions for ideas on the types of questions you may wish to ask both initially and as the relationship advances, to better understand the opportunity.

## Primary Research Questions

1. How long have you been with the Company? Where did you work before?
2. What are your primary responsibilities?
3. Tell me about your department/business unit.
4. Describe the Company's primary achievements last year.
5. What are the Company's priorities this year? How will your work/your department's work impact those priorities?
6. What trends have you identified that will impact the Company's business prospects?
7. What are the challenges your industry is facing now? How will the Company address those challenges?
8. Does the Company plan to open new offices or otherwise expand its operations this year?
9. Tell me about the Company's in-house counsel staff.
10. How many attorneys are part of the corporate counsel function? How is the unit structured? What responsibilities do they have to the Company?
11. For what purposes do you work with outside counsel?
12. How often do you retain outside counsel in the course of a typical year?
13. To which outside firms do you typically refer work? What do you particularly like about working with those firms?
14. What do you dislike most about working with outside firms?
15. What is the decision-making process for hiring outside counsel?
16. Who besides you is responsible for making decisions to hire outside counsel?

As you become more familiar with the research aspect of the business development discipline, you will find that you develop good judgment about how much time and effort to spend at the beginning of the prospecting cycle on the research and planning process for each unique contact. Less experienced business developers tend to overdo certain aspects of the secondary research and planning process early on in the business development effort with a particular contact; perhaps it is a fear of actually connecting with an individual who will be the ultimate source of opportunity. Don't be too hard on yourself when you first begin working the strategy for converting a contact into a client. As with anything, as you gain experience, your instincts will improve and you will learn how to invest time wisely and appropriately in the research and planning strategy that's key to effective business development.

Here's another aspect to this particular best practice of "Research and Plan (then repeat):" The plans you make to advance the contact relationship as a result of your initial research will need to be updated and potentially revised each time you learn more about the contact and his/her need for services. For example, when you email Sasha after the conference to let her know that you enjoyed talking with her and to send an article you wrote recently on an employer-acquirer's successor liability, you may learn that her company has just been hit with a class action employment litigation case and she intends to send out a request for proposal for representation to qualified counsel and firms within the next week. That's an unforeseen event—one that your research most likely would not have unearthed—and you will want to pivot in order to capitalize on the unexpected change in circumstances. You will want to talk with Sasha immediately—implementing a new plan—to ask if there is an opportunity for you and your firm to respond to her RFP.

The first of the five best practices instructs you that no business development plan should ever be carved in stone and slavishly pursued. Change is one of the only things you can count on in business. Do your research throughout the prospecting cycle so you may plan accordingly to use your time well and wisely in pursuit of new opportunities.

### #2: Set Realistic Goals for Advancing Relationships with Each Contact

Consider a senior associate, relatively new to business development, who identified a key contact which he considered to be one of his best opportunities for new business. He was excited because he had a telephone conference scheduled with the contact to learn more about her role as M&A counsel at a Fortune 100 company. In preparing for the conference call, he set a goal for the conversation: "I want to get her business. What an achievement it would be to bring in this company as a new client in our practice." Of course, securing the business is the ultimate goal of the prospecting phase of the business development cycle. But it is unrealistic to think that you are going to be able to close on a new business opportunity at the early stages of relationship development. An analogy would be like going on a first date with an attractive individual and asking him or her to become your life partner then and there. Every once in a while you might have a taker but usually that question would be viewed as premature, presumptuous and unwelcome. The same is true when you jump the gun with respect to your goal of working with a key contact.

Goal setting for each stage of targeting new opportunities is an essential aspect of success. For example, the senior associate's realistic goal for the initial conference call with in-house counsel should be to learn more about her responsibilities and key priorities. After learning more about her current situation, a good way to advance the relationship to the next stage might be to suggest that she attend the firm's upcoming M&A conference at which cutting-edge topics and nationally known speakers will be on the agenda. If she accepts the invitation to the conference, then the senior associate will want to develop a goal for this next phase of the business development process. Maybe that would be inviting her to dinner with some of the speakers. Not only would he get the chance to learn more about her, but indirectly he will also position the firm in a positive light by demonstrating connections in the legal and business community. Once that meeting takes place, he'll then figure out how to advance the relationship to the next logical phase of development—up to the point where it is appropriate to ask for the opportunity to work together (more on "the ask" below).

SIDEBAR: Ethical Responsibilities

Each state has a code of conduct—typically a code of professional responsibility—that governs the actions of lawyers when seeking new business and in making referrals. It is important to familiarize yourself with your state's guidelines and to adhere to them throughout the business development process. If in doubt, seek advice from a more experienced lawyer or from the firm's marketing and business development professionals.

In business development—as in all aspects of professional life—you don't always achieve the goal. The in-house counsel in the hypothetical scenario may accept the invitations to the conference and dinner, but thereafter when the associate tries to advance the relationship the response may be "radio silence." Our hypothetical associate should not take a lack of response from a key contact as evidence of personal failure. It may be that in this case, the in-house counsel's boss decided she should cultivate relationships with M&A attorneys at another firm in town (perhaps at the general counsel's former firm). Thus, despite this associate's best and most strategic efforts, his plans won't always work out. From reading the *Practical Workbook* you know that that business development is a "numbers game." A good result is converting a third of your contacts into clients. When, despite your best efforts, a particular contact goes cold, try to view it as an opportunity to promote a new contact to your Best Opportunities List and move forward with your goal setting for that prospect.

### #3: Ask for the Business

This step may seem obvious but in practice even after advancing the relationship to an appropriate point, few lawyers make it clear to prospects that they are interested in working with them. Just because you have presented a solid case on why you should be hired, you cannot leave the buying decision to chance. You really do need to ask for the business, keeping in mind any ethical restrictions.

Since this may be an awkward step and new to you, make sure you find words that will work for you.

- **Good** (and avoids any perception of ethical problems): "Let me know if there is anything I can do for you."
- **Better** (if appropriate): "I'd like to have the opportunity to work with you."
- **Best** (in proper circumstances): "How can we begin working with your company?"

Practice asking for business in low-risk situations, such as those where you have decided that there is a low likelihood you will obtain the business and you have little to lose in asking for it. You wouldn't walk into a trial without first practicing your opening statement, so you want to seek opportunities to practice how you ask for business since it is an important aspect of career success.

## #4: Ask at the Right Time

Timing is critical when asking a priority contact for business. Most lawyers over-focus on closing on a business opportunity with key contacts and fail to appreciate the critical importance of advancing the relationship to the point where it is appropriate and welcome to make the ask. As a rule of thumb, the right time to ask for business from a prospect is when you have had conversations on numerous occasions and you believe genuinely that 1) you understand the prospect's need for legal services and you view him/her as a potential asset for your practice (as described in Chapter Three); and 2) you have presented yourself as a credible and experienced resource to provide those services.

Unless you get a very clear message that the prospect is not interested in your services, seek to connect with him/her at least five times before you decide to forgo the opportunity. Recall that another aspect of the numbers game is that it takes five to ten exposures before a buying decision is made. Don't toss in the towel with a Best Opportunities contact prematurely.

Throughout the business development cycle, you need to be proactive to create the opportunity to ask for business. Here's an example: If a prospect asks for some information on your services and you send it, don't end your transmittal message with, "Please let me know if you have any questions or need additional information." You have put control of this aspect of the business development cycle into the hands of the prospect. What you need to say instead is, "I will check back to see if you have any questions or need additional information." When you contact the prospect, you are just following through—and not stalking!

## #5: Ask the Right Person

With respect to the 15 contacts you have identified as the Best Opportunities for business, think of each as belonging in one of four categories: guides, influencers, gatekeepers or decision-makers. While each may be a source of valuable opportunities, business comes only from decision-makers or with their approval. The ultimate goal of the business development cycle is to gain access to decision-makers and to avoid gatekeepers. Your guides and influencers can be helpful in gaining that access.

Let's say for example that you have identified Sid as a priority contact for a new business opportunity. Sid is the CFO at Delta Company and you assume that he has decision-making authority for hiring outside counsel for executive compensation issues. But what if he doesn't? What if in fact the general counsel or the CEO is the actual decision-maker? You may find yourself spending a lot of time and effort cultivating Sid and wondering why he isn't raising the issue of using your services.

There are some appropriate and respectful strategies for figuring out the category in which a particular contact belongs. Within the early stages of learning more about his work and his company, ask Sid a question such as, "Who besides you is involved in making decisions about hiring executive compensation counsel?" The response you receive will help you understand whether Sid is part of the decision-making team or possibly a gatekeeper whose role is to keep the uninvited out of the office of the decision-maker. Suppose that Sid, in response to your question, looks surprised and says, "Oh, the general counsel makes those decisions here. He guards that privilege closely, and rarely consults with me or others on the leadership team on the process."  Now what do you do? While less experienced business developers might end their acquaintance with Sid and seek an opportunity for an introduction to the general counsel, it's better to continue to cultivate the relationship with Sid with a changed goal or expectation. Although he is not currently part of the decision-making team, he may be a "guide" who provides more information on the process, or someone who may influence the actual decision-maker. If he likes you and finds you to be helpful, he may also agree to introduce you to the general counsel at the right time. Knowing that Sid is not the decision-maker, you recalibrate your business development strategy for Delta; maybe Delta and Sid are moved back to your B List of business development contacts. In any event, it's important to maintain a positive relationship with Sid even as you change your expectations of him.

"How's Business?"  **SIDEBAR**

This is a friendly question that your contacts may ask you at different points in the prospecting process. Give some thought to your answer because it needs to strike the right chord. If your response leads to a description of how many long hours you have worked, the vacation you missed, or the last time you saw your children in the daylight, the listener may assume you have plenty of work on your plate and if you received more, it would suffer from lack of attention. If your answer hovers at the opposite end of the spectrum and you talk about a lack of work, the listener might lose confidence in your ability, wondering why no one else is using your services. Here is an answer that will work: "Business is great but I can always handle more." Expand on that to deliver a solid reply to the question.

Having completed your reading of Chapter Five, it's time to complete your Best Opportunities List by inserting specific development strategies for each contact in the HOW column.

The sample here shows that for each contact listed, you will need to sketch out some steps to advance the relationships incrementally to the point where it is appropriate to ask for the opportunity to be of service. It's recommended that for each action step you identify, you specify a date by which you intend to complete it. This practice promotes accountability.

| WHO (Prospect Name) | WHERE (Organization) | WHAT (Describe Opportunities) | WHY (Potential Value / Likelihood of Success) | HOW/WHEN (Strategies / Dates; List at least three) |
|---|---|---|---|---|
| 1 **Jim Smith** Former Client | Now IP counsel at Acme Corp | Opportunities to work with new organization<br><br>Positive reference<br><br>Referrals to former colleagues at Beta | High Value<br><br>Medium likelihood of success | 1. Contact him by 9/15<br><br>2. Arrange meeting by 9/30<br><br>3. Follow up with invite to a program by 10/15 |
| 2 **Sally Dean** Fellow board member with American Red Cross | Attorney with Jones & Jones | Can do local counsel work for her<br><br>Her firm has no M&A attorneys | Medium Value<br><br>High likelihood of success | 1. Contact her by 9/15<br><br>2. Invite her to NAWLs meeting in October |
| 3 **Kelly Hope** Law school alum | Assistant GC at International Housewares | Opportunities to do M&A deals | Medium Value<br><br>Medium likelihood of success | 1. Contact her by 9/15<br><br>2. Send recently published article on M&A trends in October<br><br>3. Invite her to lunch in October |

*Once you have converted a contact to a client, you have to put in place a plan for maximizing your time investment in building and strengthening the relationship. Chapter Six provides guidance on how to be successful in expanding client relationships.*

- **Relationship Management with Existing Clients**
- **Ranking Your Relationships**
- **Nurturing and Cultivating Key Clients**
- **Dealing with Client Complaints as a Key Business Development Strategy**
- **How to Cross-Sell Well and Effectively**

CHAPTER SIX

# Expanding Relationships *with* Existing Clients

• • • • • • •

## Relationship Management *with* Existing Clients

Back in Chapter Two, you learned the concept that a client is a long-term strategic asset of your practice and of the firm's business. It must be clear by now that given the time and effort it takes to cultivate a prospect to the point of engagement, you want to invest not only in providing excellent substantive work product but also in managing the relationship in such a way that the client is inclined to continue to use your services. Clients are not only the source of ongoing work opportunities with their respective companies, but those who like and appreciate a law firm's services can also be referral sources and references, and may introduce you to other new work opportunities. Make sure you appreciate and actively pursue the opportunity to preserve and expand existing client relationships.

## SIDEBAR: A Prospect or a Client?

*This little story sheds light on what it means to be successful in both phases of the business development cycle.*

Upon arriving at the Pearly Gates, the most recent arrival was asked whether she wanted to spend eternity in heaven or in hell. Being an attorney in her former life, she explained to the angel that she never made a decision without first conducting due diligence and asked to have the opportunity to visit both venues before signing the eternal contract. The angel agreed and took her to heaven where everything was as she expected—peaceful, serene, clouds, angels, harps. The angel then took her to hell and the woman was quite taken aback when she saw that everyone was chic and smiling, dancing, drinking and appearing to be quite content.

She decided to sign the contract from hell. "Wow! I had no idea that hell was such a happening place! Contrary to popular belief, this is definitely the place for me!" she exclaimed.

There was paperwork to complete to close the transaction, so she went back to the Pearly Gates to sign up. Once everything was finalized, the angel escorted her back to the gates of Hell. This time, however, she smelled sulfur, saw fire and brimstone and the agony of the residents.

"What's happened?" she asked as her neat blue suit was transformed to the uniform of hellish rags.

Her angel escort smiled sweetly and paused before responding, "Well, before you were a prospect. But now you are a client. Things change!"

So the moral of this story is—and no doubt you see the facetious connection to your practice and business development efforts—make sure there is no "bait and switch" for your clients when it comes to the service you provide and your relationship development efforts. Having a "heavenly" work experience with you and your firm is key to getting more business from existing clients.

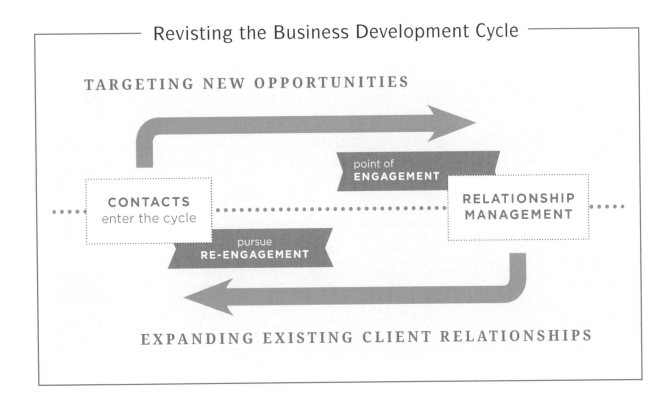

Ranking Your Relationships

Once a prospect becomes a client of your practice, you have an unequivocal obligation to provide the best advice and counsel that is possible in the circumstances. In other words, as much as possible, your substantive work must be expert and appropriate for the client you are serving, regardless of the profitability to you of that engagement or transaction. Having said that, however, not all clients have the same current or potential value as business assets of your practice or your firm.

Clients who have recurring needs for services, who are not fee-sensitive, who are loyal to you despite the efforts of your competitors to pry them away, or who are willing to be "first users" of law firm offerings—these have a high relative value to the firm. At the other extreme, clients who make only occasional use of your services or who regularly complain about fee statements, or who just don't appreciate the excellent service they receive have less value to the practice. You have an ethical obligation to serve each on the project or case you accepted, but you don't have to invest the same level of relationship management time.

To maximize your investment of time and energy in the business development process, it's important to start thinking about which clients of your practice you want to work with over and over again because they are interesting, appreciative, and profitable. You want to cultivate them actively and intentionally. Strategic and effective business development also requires that you identify clients or representative types of clients that are less than ideal in terms of work experience and profitability to your practice. These don't warrant the same type of investment.

When you are new to the business development process, it may make sense to review your billing record and matters you have worked on over a period of time and to identify those existing clients that are better targets of your client expansion efforts. In reviewing this data you may decide to assign a letter grade to each client that represents the value of the relationship to you and to the growth of your practice.

What follows is an example of how a hypothetical lawyer—let's call him Chris—ranked his existing clients from A (his best clients) to D (less valued clients).  Chris came up with criteria for ranking a client at level A, B, C or D. This is the way he described his **A-Level clients**:

- **Great to work with** (e.g., good people, trust his advice, appreciate his extra effort)
- **Interesting projects** (always something different, or testing his knowledge or expertise)
- **Profitable** clients whether at an hourly rate or on a fixed fee basis
- **Recurring work** opportunities
- **Willingness** to explore other services offered by the firm
- **Loyal** despite the efforts of competitors to win them away
- **"Cheerleaders"** for his services in the relevant community

Chris decided that if an existing client could be characterized by at least four of the criteria, it should be ranked as an A-Level client of his practice. B-Level clients exhibited fewer of these qualities and C-Level even fewer still. At the lower levels, clients were increasingly difficult to work with, offered less interesting work opportunities, and/or were fee-sensitive when it came to the firm's standard pricing. Moreover, they may also have a track record of spreading the work around to other competitor firms. While Chris recognized that his D-Level clients deserved his best substantive effort in the application of skill to serve their needs, he did not feel that the loss of their business would have a significant impact on his practice. Rather, he might be relieved if his D-Level clients walked out the door and never came back. After all, this would open up some valuable time that he could invest in expanding relationships with higher-ranked clients.

Think about whether and how this type of ranking of existing client relationships might be useful to you.  For example, if you find that a significant number of your existing clients are Bs or Cs, you might want to consider what you could do to promote them to a more valuable client of your practice. In other words, ask yourself whether you have ever explored with them the potential to expand the relationship. Be honest: Have you ever scheduled time to talk with these clients "off the meter" to determine their level of satisfaction with your current services, and to seek opportunities to do more of this work or of another type of work that they may presently send to your competitor? Another strategy for promotion might be to offer some relevant educational programming to the client contact and his colleagues, again as a value-added (and non-chargeable) service to demonstrate increased value and to promote greater loyalty.

For your A-Level clients, make sure that you are being proactive in terms of tending the relationship, demonstrating your appreciation for it, and otherwise protecting this valuable asset.

With your D-Level clients, you may find that you want to hand off some of them who occupy too much of your valuable time with their complaints, inappropriate neediness, and penny-pinching ways. By disengaging from those clients—in an ethical and appropriate way—you would have more time available to improve the quality of your current client portfolio.

| RANKING SCALE: | A= 4+ \| B= 2 or 3 \| C= 2 or 1 \| D= 1 or 0 | |
|---|---|---|
| **CLIENT** | **ATTRIBUTES** | **RANKING** |
| Acme | Great to work with; Profitable; Loyal; Cheerleader | A |
| Baker Tire | Loyal; Cheerleader | C |
| Deerfield Finance | Profitable; Recurring work opps | B |
| Juniper Construction | Interesting projects; Willingness to explore other services; Loyal | B |
| Management Magic | Great to work with; Loyal | C |
| New Life Consulting | Interesting projects; Profitable; Recurring opps; Willingness to explore other services | A |
| Open Market Ideas | Great to work with | D |
| Time Management Tools | Not sure | *not sure* |
| Southside Bank | Profitable; Willingness to explore other services | B |

Define your own criteria for determining a client's value as a business asset, or use the same criteria that Chris used. List them below.

**Attributes:**

| | |
|---|---|
| 1 _____ | 5 _____ |
| 2 _____ | 6 _____ |
| 3 _____ | 7 _____ |
| 4 _____ | 8 _____ |

*Using the attributes you have identified, rank five to ten of the clients you are working with currently or worked with recently.*

| CLIENT | ATTRIBUTES | RANKING |
|---|---|---|
| 1 | | |
| 2 | | |
| 3 | | |
| 4 | | |
| 5 | | |
| 6 | | |
| 7 | | |
| 8 | | |
| 9 | | |
| 10 | | |

# Nurturing *and* Cultivating Key Clients

What are some practical steps you can take to nurture and cultivate your A-Level clients and to promote lower ranked relationships so that their value to you increases? Here are five suggestions.

1) **Early on, make sure you establish the client's expectations of working with you.** This is purely common sense, right? You would be surprised, however, how many bright people bypass this critical strategy for nurturing an excellent client relationship. Take the lawyer, for example, who says, "I pride myself on returning all of my messages within 24 hours of receiving them." It sounds good, doesn't it? But here's the rub—if a particular client expects a call within a two-hour time frame, then this attorney has failed to meet the client's expectation.

The only way you can know what a specific client's expectations are with respect to factors such as service timeliness, budgeting, etc., is to ask. Invest time at the beginning of each client engagement (and the concept of "investment" means time you are not charging for) and ask specific questions to understand specific expectations. Don't assume that your "best practices" for service delivery or communication are going to be acceptable to a particular client. Come up with a short list of key questions you want to ask each client when you begin an engagement.

They might include:

- The manner in which they wish to receive your work product (e.g., should it be emailed or sent overnight?)
- Whether the final work product should be an oral report of recommendations or a written memo that the client may share with others in his/her organization
- The extent to which the client wants to be involved in the negotiations for the transactions
- The budget for this project
- Whether you should schedule regular status reports or be more spontaneous in communication

These are just examples of the types of issues you may raise to better understand what the client expects. The bottom line is that when you know the client's expectations in terms of service and work product, then you can focus on meeting and perhaps exceeding those expectations. Without this information, you may be setting yourself up to fail.

**2) In an appropriate way, learn more about your client contact and seek to promote his or her success.**  Most lawyers have incredible demands on their time—administrative activities, substantive work, obligations of continuing legal education, not to mention community involvement and family activities. All of these combine to make time management a challenging proposition. While you can't invest time to get to know each and every client contact of your practice, it is important to focus on building relationships with key client contacts beyond the immediate assignment. As the word connotes, "investment" means that you expect the time spent to have a significant payoff at some point. So taking a client contact out to lunch to learn more about his/her work priorities or career goals is one way to solidify the relationship and to know how you may be useful or helpful beyond the immediate assignment.

Most successful business developers take the time to inquire in an appropriate manner about clients' families and work aspirations. With this information, they can follow up to ask about a child's birthday celebration, a school graduation, and/or a new work assignment that the client contact believes will lead to a promotion. If you work on a file without taking the opportunity to get to know the person who assigns it, you are missing out on an important client-cultivation opportunity. Showing interest in others promotes a positive, influential business relationship with them. This pays dividends when the contact is in the current job situation and beyond. You want to form relationships with your clients— and in particular, with your A-Level clients —that have the potential to last over the course of your respective careers. This doesn't just happen on its own; you have to proactively manage the process.

**3) Create formal and informal "listening" opportunities.** One very successful business developer sets up a formal listening process at the beginning of each client engagement. He says to his client contact at the outset of a project, "I want to make sure that I am on track in terms of meeting your needs and serving you in the best possible way. To do this, from time to time, I am going to check in with you and ask for feedback on how I am doing. I don't want to get an A; I want to get some honest feedback to make a midcourse correction, if necessary. So, at key points in the case, I will check in with you and ask for ten or fifteen minutes of your time (not to be billed, of course) to ask specific questions about how we are doing. Is that going to be acceptable to you?"

Is there any doubt as to why this is a winning strategy for building long lasting client relationships? By setting up this dynamic at the beginning of a project, the lawyer ensures that he will hear feedback which will allow him to adjust his efforts if required. Moreover, since it is so rare for a lawyer to establish this type of feedback loop in the context of an actual client project, he guarantees that his service will stand out in a positive way from that of the competition. Think about how you might integrate this practice into your client cultivation efforts.

A less formal way of listening to clients might include tracking the company or your key contacts in the news, or regularly visiting the client's website to learn about breaking developments. A more formal approach would be to conduct client feedback surveys by arranging semiannual visits to the client's office to ask predetermined questions about the quality of service and the firm's substantive performance.

When it comes to your individual practice, there is no "one-size-fits-all" listening habit that works best for each and every client. But this should be a key part of your business development strategy. Take some time to think about what might work best for an A-Level client you wish to retain and a B-Level client you wish to promote to an A client.

4) **Develop a system for staying in touch.** Consultants David Maister and Lois Kelly published an article on Maister's website a number of years ago called, "Marketing is a Conversation." The gist of it is that to nurture existing client relationships you need to develop a system or process for staying in touch to learn about future needs, and to cultivate a relationship during the time you are "off assignment." According to this excellent article, what you want to do is come up with a calendar of key client touch points. These might include a quarterly in-house seminar program at the client's headquarters on a topic of interest, or holding regular client entertainment activities to nurture and develop the relationship.

While less valuable client relationships don't require a program of personal communication when you are between projects, your most valuable clients need to hear from you regularly and in a relevant and helpful way. After all, your most valuable clients are no doubt hearing from your competitors, and at the very least, you want to protect your flank.

5) **When the time is right, ask your clients to be your cheerleaders.** An excellent client is not only a direct source of ongoing business opportunity, but a client who is pleased with your services may also be a business-finder for you.

Every successful business developer has to be able to point to references that have experienced and appreciated his or her work. Ask your key clients who you know are satisfied with your services whether they would be willing to do this for you. Most client contacts attend professional and civic organization meetings, and generally are connected in the business sphere. If someone is well-pleased with what you have done for them, why not ask them if they would be willing to introduce you to their friends and colleagues who might have a similar legal need? Most lawyers tend to think that asking for this type of introduction is an imposition. But business people know that asking for referrals and being helpful is just part of being successful. The next time the occasion arises, and when you feel comfortable asking for one of these very important business favors, follow through. You will be pleasantly surprised by the response you receive.

# Dealing *with* Client Complaints *as a* Key Business Development Strategy

Most lawyers are individuals who experienced extraordinary academic success throughout the education process. Many pride themselves on being careful and as much as possible, perfecting the work they do for clients. So it's tough to acknowledge a shortfall. Very few mistakes will rise to the level of malpractice, but many create an irritation in the client relationship that unless addressed may lead to loss of the relationship.

Here's an example. One lawyer's important banking client referred all of its commercial loan transactions to the attorney's firm. Because the relationship was so critical, the attorney sought feedback on a regular basis with respect to both the technical quality of the work and to the delivery of the service. Over a period of time, he conducted end-of-transaction satisfaction discussions with each loan officer and identified a pattern of minor but recurring complaints about glitches in the software used by the firm to transmit confidential documents. The documents themselves were highly accurate, however, the loan officers reported consistently that they had trouble accessing them and making changes. While this problem had nothing to do with the quality of the legal work itself, if unaddressed, it could eventually lead to frustration and dissatisfaction with the firm's services. By paying attention to the key client contacts, the lawyer was able to appreciate the extent of the problem, to get it fixed by the firm's IT professionals, and to make sure that the problem was addressed to the client's satisfaction. In this case, the fix was relatively easy and in addressing it, the attorney strengthened his already positive relationship with the client. This lawyer used the client complaint process as a key business development strategy.

In your own practice, do you create the opportunity for your clients to register their complaints? Are you able to depersonalize the identification of a negative experience with you or your firm, and transform it into a business-building opportunity? The best business developers recognize that only a client who truly values the relationship will take the time to let you know when your performance falls short. Rather than avoid these discussions, they welcome them, recognizing the opportunity to take the relationship to a higher level.

If you are uncomfortable with the idea of receiving client complaints, consider Mariel's experience. A highly successful partner at her firm, Mariel agreed to take on a difficult case for one of her partner's clients. At the time, Mariel was not aware that her partner had negotiated a fixed-fee arrangement with the client. She worked hard on the matter and tracked all of her time as she would in a traditional hourly-billing arrangement. When it came time to generate the monthly bill, her partner was on an extended vacation so she handled the bill for him. A few days after the bill was sent, she received a very angry call from the client contact. Not only was he irate at receiving a bill that was well beyond the amount he had anticipated, he also took the opportunity to question a number of the activities itemized in the billing statement, of which he had not been aware. He ended the call by saying, "When Jim gets back, I am going to talk to him about transitioning this case to another firm. A competent lawyer would not have sent me such an inappropriate billing statement and some of the steps you have taken just don't seem necessary to me at all."

A perfectionist by nature and an extremely service-oriented individual, Mariel was devastated by the client's complaints. She called her partner on vacation and told him what had happened. At the same time she suggested to him that she would take full responsibility for the situation, and endeavor to make it right. This story has a happy ending: Mariel waited a few days and then asked the client if she could make a visit to his office to learn more about his concerns in an effort to fix the problems. She took full responsibility for the billing issues, apologized sincerely, and spent two hours at his office listening to what some might consider to be the client's "silly" complaints. She asked the client how he wished her to address his concerns and promised to take prompt action. That was six months ago. Since that time, the client contact has sent two more cases to Mariel with the request that she handle them personally. Further, he has told Jim and others in the firm that Mariel is a rare type of professional person—honest, non-defensive, and willing to admit to her mistakes. He also told the firm that this is exactly the type of person he wants handling his work now and in the future.

TAKE 5: **Talk with Attorneys about Their Personal Experience**

Think about your typical response to work-related criticism. Do you tend to get angry and defensive when someone makes a negative remark about your work in an effort to help you improve? Are you comfortable asking questions to better understand what to do differently in the future? Regardless of your natural reaction, in business situations try to stay calm and focused on what you may learn from a client or a colleague's criticism. Be careful not to burn bridges because you feel emotional. What did you do the last time you received constructive criticism? Did you build the relationship with your critic as a result of your response? Did you damage the relationship by your reaction? Be honest, and if your behavior had the potential to harm your business relationship, think of how you may act differently the next time you receive less than positive performance feedback.

# How *to* Cross-Sell Well *and* Effectively

Cross-selling is the practice of expanding the range and nature of services that a firm provides for an existing client. If the banking practice group provides loan documents for a financial institution, there may be litigation opportunities with the same target. When you undertake the cross-selling practice, you approach the bank and relevant decision-makers to offer the firm's litigation services which they have not used before but may be well disposed to, given the client's long-term and satisfactory relationship with the loan documentation practice area.

You would think that any multi-practice law firm would have a robust and successful cross-selling initiative as a key strategy to expand existing client relationships. But it often doesn't work that way. One of the most difficult sales strategies for lawyers to get comfortable with is the process of cross-selling. Because of the challenges it poses, it seldom gets off the ground. As a result, many law firms are losing opportunities to cultivate and expand existing client relationships.

The main reason that cross-selling can be difficult has to do with attorneys' natural tendencies to want to protect key client relationships they have developed and nurtured over time. The fear is that a colleague who has the expertise the client needs (but is unfamiliar with the relationship and the players) may inadvertently cause harm to a valuable asset of an individual lawyer's practice. Unless an attorney has a particularly positive experience with a colleague's cross-selling efforts, he/she might naturally assume "no one can take better care of the client than me" or even worse, "this person could totally screw up the positive relationship I've built with this particular client."

How can you overcome some of the understandable obstacles to cross-selling? Here are some best practices:

1) **Get to know colleagues in other practice areas of the firm before the opportunity to cross-sell arises.** Getting to know your colleagues off assignment includes understanding their pet peeves when it comes to the practice of law, appreciating their style and approach to client work, and having a sense of their goals for developing their individual practices. At the same time, your colleagues will get to know you as an engaged professional and realize you share many of the same values around client service and other aspects of work. When the time comes to talk specifically about cross-selling together, you will have laid a positive and influential foundation for a fruitful discussion.

2) **Demonstrate that you are a trustworthy caretaker of other attorneys' client relationships.** Let's say that a firm colleague in a different practice group agrees to introduce you to one of his/her key client relationships for the purpose of discussing the use of your services. This is an important moment, and you need to demonstrate in word and by your actions that you appreciate the importance of the client relationship, that you understand your colleague's goals for developing it, and that you will be a trustworthy collaborator in that process.

Strategies for demonstrating this would include:

- Advising your colleague of your communications with the client contact in an accurate and complete way

- Reinforcing the client's positive relationship with your colleague by speaking of your colleague in highly positive terms and complimenting the client's choice of him/her as a service provider

- If applicable, talking with your colleague in a candid and above-board manner about the allocation of billing credit for new client matters and projects, and making sure that you resist an inclination to seek credit when it is not due

- Touching base with your colleague on a regular basis to make sure he/she has no concerns about the manner in which you are serving the client or on any other issues related to your work

3) **Initiating cross-selling opportunities with clients of your practice.** Most lawyers want to be the recipient of colleagues' efforts to cross-sell their services to existing clients, but few focus on the importance of introducing trusted colleagues to their own client relationships. As you build influential relationships with your attorney colleagues at the firm, be sure to inquire about the types of clients they seek, the projects they are best-suited to work on, etc. Let trusted colleagues know that you are willing to introduce them as appropriate to clients that may need their services. By initiating cross-selling opportunities on behalf of your colleagues, you'll demonstrate the kind of mutuality and trust-worthiness that promotes a reciprocal effort from them.

It takes an investment of time and effort first in connection with your colleagues within the firm and then with external clients to make cross-selling an effective client-expansion strategy. Once the practice catches hold, however, it can positively impact a firm's client expansion results and its culture. It will help you to develop more positive relationships with your generational peers within the firm and create a platform for building a sustaining practice.

*Now that you have invested time in defining target contacts and building existing client relation-ships, you need to learn the best practices for conducting sales meetings during each stage of the business development cycle. While preparation is a key element in the success of a sales meeting, how you conduct the meeting is equally important. In Chapter Seven, you will learn how to prepare for a sales event, conduct it, and follow up to win or expand the business.*

- **Preparing for a Sales Meeting**
- **Conducting a Sales Meeting with Prospects and with Existing Clients**
- **Following Up After the Sales Meeting**
- **Other Considerations**

CHAPTER SEVEN

# Conducting *a* Successful Sales Meeting

● ● ● ● ● ● ● ●

At several points in the business development cycle—whether you are prospecting for new op-portunities or seeking to expand client relationships—you will be in a position to conduct a sales meeting. Not every sales meeting is a formal event, involving a "dog-and-pony-show" type of effort, but each requires an appropriate amount of preparation, a strategy for managing the sales meeting itself, and follow-up activities focused on bringing in the business. Because you are the one who wants the business, it is your job to understand the sales meeting process and to manage it. While there are attorneys who bumble their way through sales meetings and end up getting the business anyway, a greater number miss out on new business opportunities because they don't understand how to prepare for and conduct an effective sales session. In Chapter Seven, you will learn how to prepare for a sales event, conduct it and follow up to win the business.

# Preparing *for a* Sales Meeting

Let's say that you receive a call from a prospective client, Sam, who says you were recommended to him by your long-time client, Linda. Sam is the owner of a mid-sized private company and has been named as a defendant in an unexpected lawsuit. He tells you that on Linda's recommendation, he would like to set up a meeting with you to determine if you are the right person to represent him in what he describes as a messy and distressing business dispute. At the end of the week, Sam will meet with you for 90 minutes at your office to talk about his situation and to learn more about your credentials to provide counsel.

As you progress in practice, this will start to be a more typical occurrence—assuming you have developed your skills in an excellent way and have been networking with business colleagues, seeking their introductions to new opportunities. It is hard to know at this point—in this hypothetical and when this type of event actually arises in your practice—whether Sam's call and the upcoming meeting with him represent a "golden moment of opportunity" for you to obtain a new client and do the work that you have come to enjoy.

How do you prepare for the meeting with Sam in such a way that allows you to put your best foot forward with him and to win the opportunity eventually? At the same time that you seek to impress him with your experience and ability, how will you assess whether this is the type of case and client that will help you build your practice and credentials? Here are some recommended steps to take.

## Conduct primary research

Lawyers are trained to conduct research and it's a comfort zone for most. Typically, however, when it comes to business development opportunities they spend too much time on secondary research and too little time focusing on primary resources.

In this case, the first piece of primary research to undertake is to call Linda, the person who recommended you to Sam. You want to do this for a number of good reasons. First, Linda has performed a business favor for you in referring Sam as a potential client and you need to thank her. This step is imperative whether you get the work or not; showing your appreciation is an important aspect of relationship-building and one of the ways that you promote Linda's willingness to keep looking for new opportunities for you. Next, you will ask Linda how she came to refer Sam to you in connection with this case. Find out how she knows him, and what she knows about his business. When you ask these types of questions—especially if you have first expressed your gratitude for the referral—it is likely Linda will provide you with some excellent and useful information that will help you understand Sam's circumstances and give you a sense as to whether he will be a good client for you.

For example, what if in response to your questions Linda says, "Oh, Sam is my brother-in-law's friend. I don't really know much about him or his business. I was just doing my brother-in-law a favor by telling him who we work with in litigation matters"? Then you know Sam is something of a "wild card" when it comes to the opportunity presented. Also, it's likely that if you decide not to work with him you won't be offending Linda. You may also be dodging a bullet in terms of acquiring a potential D-Level client as described in Chapter Six.

On the other hand, when you call to ask for more information Linda may tell you, "Sam is one of our key vendors and he is a great guy. We have done business with him for years and he runs such a tight operation that he rarely finds himself in situations such as this one. He has been very successful to date and I know this dispute is devastating to him. I hope you will be able to help him." Clearly, if Linda makes the latter response, you have a sense that this may be an excellent opportunity; after all, Linda is a great client of yours and if she speaks so highly of Sam, then no doubt it's likely that you will want to work with him. Do you see how the intelligence you receive from Linda—whatever it is—shapes the way you approach the sales situation with Sam?

Another aspect of primary research to be conducted prior to the actual meeting will be to ask Sam some additional questions so you can prepare well for the in-person session. Here are some additional items you may wish to ask to develop your strategy for the sales discussion:

- What are Sam's specific goals for the discussion? They may range from getting some free legal advice to helping him decide if you are the type of person—in terms of your communication style, demeanor, experience, etc.—to represent him in what he considers to be a high stakes and personally upsetting situation.

- Is anyone else from the business attending the meeting with him? If so, what role will that person or persons have in the case?

- Are there materials he would like you to review in advance of the meeting, such as a copy of the complaint or documents that are the basis for the dispute?

- You should assume that he is talking with other potential counsel—and it is appropriate to ask if that is the case—and if yes, inquire as to which other firms and attorneys he is meeting. Why is it important to gather this information? Because if he is speaking only with you, then the opportunity is yours to win or lose. Your strategy in the sales meeting may be more direct than if you know that there are other attorneys he is also interviewing. If he is meeting with your competitors, knowing who they are will help you to emphasize your competitive strengths as part of the sales meeting.

SIDEBAR: Your Competitor

It may go without saying, but never criticize a competitor in front of a potential client. It won't help you win the business and it is potentially insulting to the prospect's judgment. After all, the prospect has decided to interview the other attorney and by making negative comments about the competition you are indirectly criticizing your potential client.

## Do some secondary research

This research will include obtaining company information and reviewing the biographies of key players in the case or transaction. There is so much information available online and through proprietary databases that you may find yourself overwhelmed with data. Remember that a sales meeting is not a test of how well you researched the opportunity, the players and the industry. A sales meeting is an opportunity for counsel and prospective clients to take each other's measure and decide if there is a good fit between the lawyer and the lawyer's capabilities, experience, and personal style and the needs of the prospective client. Asking our hypothetical prospect, Sam, to describe his goals for the meeting as part of the primary research will also help you to put parameters around the type and extent of secondary research it would be helpful to conduct in advance of the meeting. Ask your firm's marketing professionals for help and advice with this aspect of preparation.

## Prepare your questions

The meeting structure described below contemplates that before talking in some detail about your qualifications and experience to represent the prospect, you will first conduct a brief and friendly interview of the prospect to develop a better understanding of the need for counsel as well as the decision-making process for selecting representation. In the same way that you have strategy for depositions, negotiating transactions, and other aspects of your substantive practice, you want to think through in advance what you need to know from the prospect to clarify the business opportunity and to be in a position to describe your own and the firm's capabilities in a persuasive way. So let's go back to our scenario with prospective client Sam. Based on the research you've conducted thus far, here are a few items you may wish to ask him at the in-person meeting:

- Can you tell me more about your business and how this particular dispute arose?
- Ideally, how would you like to see this case resolved? Why?
- What do you know about the litigation process?
- What are your priorities for this case and the way it will be managed? Will you be your counsel's primary point of contact or will someone else in the company take primary responsibility?
- Have you given any thought to a budget for the company's defense? Do you have insurance that may cover some or all of the legal fees and costs?
- What will the decision-making process be for selecting outside counsel and what is the timing for it?

There's no cookie-cutter formula for the specific questions you should ask at a particular sales meeting. What will be helpful and useful to ask depends on the facts of each situation. Put your "strategy cap" on and spend time preparing the questions to ask different prospective clients in order to better understand their respective situations and to determine how to win the work.

## Create a brief presentation

In preparing for a sales meeting or similar type of conversation, you have limited information to work with; after all, one of the main reasons for conducting a sales meeting is to better understand the prospect's situation and to present yourself and your firm as the best resources to address it. Still, you want to consider in advance what features of your practice and experience you believe—based on what you know now—will most benefit the prospective client. After the interview phase of the sales meeting, you will make your presentation in a conversational and responsive way.

Attorneys who are inexperienced business developers tend to view the entire purpose of a sales meeting as an opportunity to make a presentation—talking most of the time about themselves, the firm, the firm's honors and recognitions, and using PowerPoint slides to make each and every one of their points—in a way that may be totally disconnected from the prospect's specific concerns. In fact and depending on how formal the sales meeting is intended to be, you should limit your presentation to 30 percent of the time allotted for the entire meeting. Unless the meeting is very formal or you have some technical information to present, don't use a visual presentation. If you think that slides or diagrams may be useful to illustrate some complex points you wish to make, then print out a slide deck or diagrams for the prospect to review in connection with your comments.

## Think about objections or other challenges that may be raised

When a prospective client questions whether your credentials or experience are suited to the needs in a particular case or matter, take heart. Rather than viewing a "sales objection" as a challenge or worse, as an insult, consider it an opportunity to be helpful and to educate. Think about it: When you prepare to make a purchase or to retain a professional, typically you are going to ask questions to make sure that you are selecting the right resource, the one that will address your specific purchasing needs. The same is true with prospective clients of your practice. When they ask questions or raise what sound like objections to working with you, it's best to stay calm, probe a bit to better understand the concern, and address it directly and truthfully. As part of your preparation for the sales session, think through the types of tough questions or objections that may be raised by the prospect and consider how you will respond.

**If others will be invited, give them a role**

It's not uncommon for an associate attorney to invite a more senior attorney or a partner to join a sales meeting. At some firms you may be required to have a partner participate. In certain situations it makes sense to invite a colleague or colleagues to join the meeting, especially when it appears that you may not have the precise experience or skill to address the prospect's needs or concerns.

If you do invite colleagues to join you for the sales meeting, consider the following preparatory steps:

- Everyone who joins the sales meeting should play an active role in it. When you are in charge of the opportunity, it's up to you to consider who should be invited to the meeting and the sales task to be assigned to each participant.
- Let the prospective client know in advance if anyone other than you will participate in the meeting and explain why. Don't spring a sales team on a prospect on the day of the meeting. This may undermine your credibility and the prospect may view it as a potential "bait and switch" in terms of who may actually be working on the case or matter. As David Maister wrote in his excellent article, "How Clients Choose," prospective clients tend to be worried and concerned when they meet with counsel for the first time (especially when litigation is involved), so be sure to explain your choice of a presentation team as a matter both of courtesy and to minimize the prospect's potential anxiety.
- Practice your respective roles before the sales meeting. This should go without saying. Who goes into court without talking through an oral argument? What attorney goes into a negotiation without jotting down the key points she wants to make? A sales meeting with a prospective client should be no different. If colleagues don't have time for a rehearsal, consider replacing them on the team. It's that important!

TAKE **5** : Sales Meetings

Think about the last time you were involved—either directly or tangentially—in preparing for a sales meeting. What were the circumstances? What aspects of preparation described above did you undertake to get ready for the sales meeting? Did you end up getting the business? Based on what you know now about preparing for sales meetings, what would you have done differently to prepare? Do you think it may have made a difference with respect to the outcome of the opportunity?

# Conducting *the* Sales Meeting

Sales meetings typically have four discrete parts as follows: introduction, prospective client interview, presentation, and closing. This is true with both formal and informal sales discussions.

The purpose of the **introduction** is to set the proper tone for the meeting, including confirming the goals for the session, and to establish peerage with the prospect.

When it takes place at your office, consider yourself the host of the sales meeting. A host makes sure that guests are comfortable, offers refreshments, and facilitates necessary introductions.

What does it mean to establish "peerage" as part of the introduction? This is a subtle but important strategy. In medieval times, it was only appropriate for peers to interact as equals, and this concept survives in our current business culture. One reason that you may sometimes invite a "grey hair" or "no hair" senior colleague to attend sales meetings is a sense that you are not the peer in experience or seniority of the general counsel or other client representative with whom you'll be meeting. Attorneys and other business people who have a youthful appearance—despite their age and experience—sometimes make a humorous remark to assure new acquaintances they have the necessary expertise to run a sales meeting and the subsequent case or transaction that may result from it (e.g., "Just so you know, I have been practicing law here for the past ten years and there was no violation of child labor laws involved with my employment.").

In the case of our hypothetical sales meeting with Sam, 90 minutes have been allocated for the entire session. Ten percent of that time will typically be spent on the introduction so in this situation, no more than 10 minutes of the total time allotted for the meeting.

The next stage of the sales meeting is the **interview**. During the interview you explore the new business opportunity by using open-ended questions that you have prepared in advance. The point is to get as much information as possible from the prospective client about concerns and priorities for a particular case or matter so that you can assess the type of opportunity it presents. Just as in the deposition of a friendly witness, you'll start with broader questions and clarify the situation by following up with more specific items that you may not have anticipated asking. To prepare for the prospective client interview, consider the questions listed below and use those that are most appropriate to develop your understanding of the client's need for service. About 40 percent of the time you spend at the sales meeting should be devoted to the prospective client interview. This may seem like a lot of time, but it's critical to establishing rapport with the prospective client and to exploring the opportunity thoroughly. Remember those D-Level clients described in Chapter Six? You want to avoid getting yourself into one of those relationships. You also want to better understand how to put your best foot forward in the next stage of the sales meeting. The only way to accomplish both of these objectives is to ask questions and elicit helpful information from the prospect.

## Client Interview Questions

1. We've talked generally already about the case/transaction for which you're seeking counsel. Is there any new information that I should be aware of or that you would like to share with me?
2. Describe the outcomes you're seeking in this case/transaction.
3. Is this a unique case/transaction for the company? What is the company's prior experience with this type of case/transaction? What were the outcomes of prior cases/transactions?
4. What is your budget for the services of outside legal counsel?
5. [If there is in-house/corporate counsel at the prospective client] How do you see our firm partnering with corporate counsel?
6. What's your timetable for this case/transaction?
7. What are some of your pet peeves about working with outside counsel? What are some best practices that you have established for working with outside counsel that you would like us to be aware of?
8. Who besides you will be working with outside counsel on this case/transaction? Describe how you anticipate that outside counsel will interact with you and your colleagues.
9. How will you ultimately make the decision regarding retention of outside counsel? What are your priorities in that regard? What is the timetable for the decision-making process?
10. Do you have any specific questions or issues that you would like me to address as part of our discussion today?

The **presentation** is the third stage of the sales meeting. Prior to the meeting, you will prepare a brief presentation that you will deliver in a conversational way following the interview phase of the sales session. But be prepared to pivot away from your original text based on what you learn in the interview. You want to weave into your presentation the concerns and issues you learn about in the interview, and describe why you and the firm may be the best choice to resolve them. Remember to restrict yourself to 30 percent of the meeting time for your presentation, a portion of which will be spent responding to the prospect's "objections."

The single greatest mistake that lawyers tend to make in sales meetings is to fail to close—either at all, or in an effective way. The **closing** is the fourth and final stage of the sales meeting, and its purpose is to establish the next step in the sales process—not necessarily to ask for the business. The closing step in the sale process depends entirely on how urgent the prospect's need is for assistance, where the prospect is in the decision-making process, and a variety of other factors that you will understand better as a result of the interview and presentation process. It is your task to find out what the next logical step in the sales process will be and to make it happen. The next step may include one of the following activities:

- Providing the prospect with more information about specific services
- Setting up a subsequent meeting with others from the company to talk further
- Beginning a conflict check to make sure you and the firm are in a position to represent the prospect
- Drafting an engagement letter for review by the prospect
- Offering specific client references for the prospect to contact for information about your services
- Getting hired and starting work on the engagement

Never leave a sales meeting without establishing the next step in the sales process. If it doesn't suggest itself to you as a result of your discussions with the prospect then say: "It's been a pleasure to meet with you today. May I ask where we go from here?" In some cases—as with Sam in our example, who has little or no experience with selecting litigation counsel to defend him—the prospect may not know what he or she will do next as part of the sales process. If you have this sense, then make a recommendation. You may say something like, "I know this is a tough situation for you. Let me give you a few days to think about the next step. May I call you on Friday if I don't hear from you by then to find out how you would like to proceed?"

Allocate 20 percent of the meeting time for the closing stage.

## Structure of a Sales Meeting

| Intros 10% | Interview 40% | Presentations 30% | Closing 20% |
|---|---|---|---|

# Following Up After *the* Sales Meeting

After investing significant time and effort preparing for and conducting the sales meeting, be sure to follow up and complete the next step in the sales process that you established at the close of the sales session. Don't drop the ball at this point. Follow through with agreed upon next steps, and then ask again, "Where do we go from here?" If you are disciplined and intentional about pursuing a new business opportunity to its logical conclusion, your sales meeting success will start strong and continue to improve over time.

# Other Considerations

**If you don't get the work**

What if you do everything well and effectively in the sales effort and you find out you are not selected for the case or project? Salvage the time spent on the sales process by conducting a forensic analysis. Ask your contact who was chosen to provide representation and what the determining factors were in the decision-making process. More than half of the time you'll find that contacts appreciate the time and effort you spent trying to win their business and they'll readily provide you with this information. Why is it important to ask? Mainly to find out about your competition's advantage—at least as it was perceived by this prospect. It may suggest to you what you need to emphasize in future sales opportunities to win the business. Asking for this information may also confirm to you that the prospect was probably not the right fit for you and your firm, and you may be able to use that information in sizing up future new business opportunities.

## When responding to a request for proposal

Here are some rules to follow when responding to a formal request for proposal for legal services from a client or prospect:

- Determine whether it's a real opportunity or if you are being positioned as a "stalking horse" so that the prospect may extract concessions from its current counsel. The only way to do this is to ask to speak with the prospective client representative and to pose the same types of open-ended questions appropriate to the client interview stage of a sales meeting.

- If the prospect is not willing to provide you with information about the opportunity and the purpose of the RFP, you may decide that it's not a particularly good opportunity for you and your firm. Don't think you have to respond to all requests for proposals. Be strategic in how you assess the opportunity and invest time responding.

- Speak with firm leaders and marketing professionals to obtain their input on the opportunity. This may be the first time that you've received an RFP, but the firm has institutional experience regarding such contests. Ask for help and advice in assessing the opportunity, and if you decide to go forward and respond, in preparing the response.

- Assuming you decide to respond to the RFP, do an excellent job on it. Your response is an example of your own and your firm's work product and may be viewed as a proxy for your actual legal representation. Provide a timely response in the way requested by the prospect. Address each and every item, in the order and format indicated. Don't try to stand out from the crowd by varying from the requested information or format; this strategy will probably backfire and cause you to be eliminated from consideration.

## Conflict checks

Each firm has its own policies regarding the conflict-checking process and the types of clients or matters that it does not wish to pursue. Get to know those policies and procedures before you have a live sales opportunity. This will save you time and energy pursuing opportunities that the firm will not ultimately approve because of conflict concerns.

**Firm policies about new client engagements**

Does the firm have a standard engagement letter that must be issued as part of the client retention process? Are retainer fees charged to clients that are new to the firm? Again, find out about standard practices before you find yourself in a sales situation. Ask under what circumstances—if any—the standard policies may be varied. You want to be sure that when prospective clients ask questions about the terms of engagement you are prepared to respond. This is an aspect of the business of law that must be considered if your goal is to become increasingly more proficient and successful in business development.

*Your "personal brand" identifies and distinguishes you from other providers of legal services. You need to be mindful of and manage the elements that combine to define your brand. Chapter Eight takes you through a check list of those elements and how they relate to your brand.*

- **Developing a Personal Commercial**
- **Crafting and Managing Your Professional Profile**
- **Key Aspects of Brand Management**

CHAPTER EIGHT

# Managing Your Brand

• • • • • • • •

Brand is the name, term, design, symbol, or any other feature that identifies one seller's goods or services and distinguishes those goods or services from other sellers' products or offerings. Brand management seeks to make the service relevant to and consistent in the eyes of the target market. Personal branding treats individuals and their careers as a brand (think Oprah Winfrey, for example).

In Chapter One, where the difference between marketing and business development is discussed, there is a description of the four Ps of marketing. You will recall that the target market, however you define it, is the focal point for all of your efforts and initiatives to build business. One aspect of marketing, referred to as "promotion," includes not only the sales-related business development activities that have been described up to this point in the *Practical Workbook* but also the concept of branding. As described above and applied to a lawyer's practice, branding means the totality of an individual attorney's efforts to raise his or her profile to build visibility and to use those activities to connect with the target market.

This chapter focuses on how to assess and implement various aspects of professional brand management—including the development of a "personal commercial," involvement in organizations and community groups, use of articles and speeches, and other promotional tactics—in a consistent way to define and promote your brand. While most law firms employ professionals to manage the overall brand of the organization, individual lawyers have to do that for themselves. Because your brand becomes the platform from which you develop business, the sooner you begin to manage it well and strategically, the greater the opportunities will be for person-to-person business development.

## Developing a Personal Commercial

An attorney's personal commercial (also known as an "elevator speech") is a powerful and compelling statement about who you are, what you do, and why the message is important to the listener. Typically, these statements are used in professional networking settings and in more formal contexts such as sales meetings and speech introductions. Calling it a "commercial" conveys just how short and punchy it needs to be. And just as with consumer-focused commercials, you need to make certain the message is appropriate for the specific audience you are addressing.

As mentioned throughout the *Practical Workbook*, an attorney wouldn't dream of making his or her first oral argument without first writing it down and rehearsing it. The same probably applies to rehearsing the questions for the first time he or she takes a deposition. The questions are written out and most lawyers—whether they will admit it or not—practice those questions orally and in front of the mirror. In the same way, it is imperative to write down your personal commercial (in a couple of different versions for different types of settings) and to practice saying it. You want to be sure that your message, though brief, is ready for prime time and reflects a comfortable and natural way of speaking, both for you and your target audience.

Before you start, here is one quick test for a commercial: If you can change the name of the attorney/firm, and the message still works, then your commercial is not ready for airing. An example: "I am an associate with Great Law. The firm has three offices and 150 attorneys in Indiana." Looking at this example (be honest, you have used something similar yourself), consider the following:

- Do you need to say "associate"? Not if attorney works just as well. Save the use of a title for later.
- Is the name of the firm important? Yes, because it immediately associates you with anything the listener knows about the firm (and if you are not comfortable with that, maybe you are with the wrong firm).
- Is the number of offices important? Not really.
- Is the number of attorneys important? Not really, especially since it will create an instant reaction of too big or too small since size is an easy attribute for anyone to relate to.
- Is location important? Not really unless it is directly related to the legal services you provide. (An example would be when talking with the representative of an international corporation where worldwide capabilities would be important and of interest.)

Here are elements that should be a part of your commercial:

- A statement of what you do in terms that are meaningful to the listener; keep it simple and don't load it up with legal jargon unless your listener's ear is tuned to it
- A description of the value your work provides to the listener
- A focus on key firm selling points that differentiate the firm
- A reference to how many years you have been practicing law (if it would be impressive/helpful to the listener)
- A memorable hook—something that would perk up the listener's ears

## TAKE 5: Reviewing Commercials

Here is an example of a personal commercial. Read it through and then evaluate it. Did it pique your interest? Would you remember this person? How would you improve upon it?

*As an employment attorney at Smith & Smith, I help companies develop human resource policies to limit disputes and claims from employees. With the downturn in the economy, I have been providing more counseling on reduction in force issues over the past year than I have in the entire 15 years I have been practicing law.*

What about this one? How would you improve this commercial?

*I represent companies in connection with major transactions ranging from one hundred million to over a billion dollars in value. As partner with the firm, I can bring to bear the resources of more than 800 attorneys in 14 offices located throughout the U.S., Europe, and Asia.*

Here's another to consider. How would you improve this commercial?

*I am a commercial litigation attorney, representing some of the region's most significant companies when disputes arise. I just settled a case for a client involving a software licensing dispute with a million dollars at stake; this is typical of my practice though I also handle other types of business litigation throughout the Midwest.*

| EXERCISE | Personal Commercials |
|---|---|
| | *Write and Practice Two Personal Commercials for Yourself* |
| | 1 |
| | |
| | |
| | 2 |
| | |
| | |

# Crafting *and* Managing Your Professional Profile

What do you want to be when you "grow up"? Create a vision in your mind and consider all the elements it will take to develop into that professional person. It is important to hold onto the vision when making decisions regarding the legal matters you take on and business development activities. Your time is not limitless so every action you take should be effective in achieving your vision. As you construct your professional profile over time, it becomes the basis for one of the most important written products in your business development tool box—your biography, bio or profile. The biography section of law firm websites is by far the most frequently accessed data. You need to make certain your bio is crisp, complete, and well-written. Many firms have a marketing staff that is responsible for creating and maintaining bios and is likely to have guidelines on how to write them. Make certain you are satisfied with what is included in your biography and that you remember to continually update it (e.g., speaking engagements, new experience, published articles). Even if your firm automatically adds these items to attorney bios, review yours from time to time to make sure the edits are accurate.

## TAKE 5: Review the Profile of an Attorney (Outside Your Firm)

What does a good profile look like? Go to a competitor's website and pull up the bio of a leading partner. What does it tell you about him or her? What does it tell you if you read between the lines?

As an example: *"Mr. Olson (Theodore Olson of Gibson Dunn & Crutcher) was Solicitor General of the United States prior to joining the firm."* You know from reading just this line that this lawyer is a player, understands politics, is influential, and that it speaks well for the firm to be in a position to attract such an accomplished lawyer. It's taken Ted Olson a lifetime of law practice to achieve the credentials featured in his professional profile, but at some point he had a vision of how he wanted to shape his future and his brand. As you review other well-known attorneys' professional profiles, think about the strategy each is employing to develop credentials that promote a certain brand.

Ask yourself: "What should I be doing now and in the future to manage my brand with my key target markets?"

# Key Aspects *of* Brand Management

Brand management is the term used to describe the business development activities in which you engage in order to build or develop a certain brand with relevant target markets. Back in Chapter One we discussed Timothy Leishman's "Sustaining Practice Styles" and noted that individual attorneys may build business using different styles based on natural personality traits and target market considerations. As you review the activities described below, think about the Sustaining Practice Style you identified with and also the types of brand development activities that will connect you with relevant targets. Over time and with practice, the idea is to arrive at a promotional mix that is comfortable for you as well as meaningful to current and potential clients.

## Professional or Industry Organizations

*Key Objective:* Develop your professional network outside the firm, and build your brand with specific referral sources and prospective clients.

Some firms are generous in supporting lawyers' memberships in professional organizations, such as bar associations and industry-specific groups like the Urban Land Institute, the American Hospital Association, the Society of Licensing Executives, etc. Confirm your firm's policy and take full advantage of appropriate memberships. If your firm does not cover membership dues, make the personal investment in your career and pay the dues. Consider involvement in those associations and organizations that will provide the greatest brand and business development opportunities with your key target markets. If you join an organization, attend its meetings and events and network actively. If you find over time that participating in the group is not serving the purposes you had hoped, then make a change.

To raise your profile with a particular group you will want to join a committee and get on the leadership ladder. One of the best committees to join is the program committee. It affords the opportunity to reach out to just about anyone when seeking presenters for a program plus it provides visibility at the program itself, with at a minimum, recognition in the program book and possibly as a moderator or presenter. Participating on the membership committee is also a good way to connect with new contacts.

**Community Groups**

*Key Objective:* Enhance your network of non-attorney contacts and make a civic contribution to a cause in your local community.

There are two approaches to involvement in community groups for you to consider. First is to identify a group whose purpose relates to a community cause or issue that you believe in and wish to support with your personal efforts. In this case, you decide to use your professional stature to work with organizational colleagues to achieve a common goal in your community. Whether you join the local chapter of Habitat for Humanity, the Young Friends of the Symphony or a social justice organization, it creates the opportunity to harness the passion you have for the cause with your professional skills and connections. Many attorneys find that this combination is powerful in building a positive brand with members and constituents of the organization they join and it often connects them with client opportunities.

Another approach is to consider service on the board of a community group. Many communities have an organization that serves as a clearinghouse for matching board positions and people seeking to volunteer for them; it may be the best starting point for you. Another resource: Tap attorneys in your firm who currently serve on local boards. They may be helpful in introducing you to the organization's leadership and possibly in securing you a position on a committee.

Volunteering for a community organization allows you to meet like-minded individuals while making a valuable contribution of time and talent. Depending on your role, it can also provide opportunities you are unlikely to encounter in your day job, for example, writing text for the organization's website or leading a key development initiative. The objective is a leadership position where you can demonstrate your skills at strategic thinking, problem solving and team management. Your performance in the organization is critical since others can use it to judge you and form an opinion of your work.

## SIDEBAR: Protecting Your Brand

Be careful about the "brand" you project. Getting involved in organizations—whether as a leader, a member, or a worker bee—may be an excellent way to build your brand and meet significant business contacts. But keep in mind, too, that your behavior and level of engagement will be viewed potentially as a "proxy" for what it may be like to work with you professionally.

For example, Suzette joins the local board of her community's food bank because it is a cause she believes in strongly, and she also wants to begin raising her profile with the local professional community. She is often late for board meetings because of her demanding schedule, and while there, she is often observed reading messages on her phone, emailing, and texting. She rarely participates in the discussions at meetings and sometimes seems to be dozing off during them. Whether she is aware of it or not, her lack of engagement in the meetings is negatively perceived by her board colleagues who take the work very seriously. Suzette would most likely be shocked to realize that her conduct at organizational events is actually creating a negative brand—i.e., it is a potential proxy for the type of behavior that she would demonstrate in a professional work setting. In this case, it would be better for Suzette to quit the board and spend more time at work rather than risk harming her professional reputation by her unengaged behavior.

**Writing Articles**

*Key Objective:* Build your profile as an expert.

Writing articles is an ideal way to build your profile as an expert. You do not need to write an article worthy of publication in a law journal unless your audience is the legal community and your preference is to develop a more scholarly reputation. Instead, consider targeting publications read by potential clients. If your law firm has resources to help with article placement (e.g., marketing department professionals, public relations firm), start there to research publications and topics. Do not start by writing an article and sending it to several editors. A better strategy is to solve a problem for an editor by providing him/her with an article idea and explaining why the publication's readers will find it of value. The editor then has an opportunity to share with you the length, the due date, and possible other issues to include in the discussion. Review issues of targeted publications to be certain the topic has not been covered in recent editions or in a competing media outlet.

One of your objectives is to be able to recycle your article after it is published by emailing it to contacts, using it as a handout at presentations, posting it on the firm's website, creating a podcast based on it, or including it in new business pitch materials. Make certain the publication gives you the rights to use the article without having to pay; reprint rights can be expensive. Do not distribute it in the format you submitted to the publication (i.e., Word document, Times Roman font, etc.). Instead, ask to receive a PDF from the publisher, or create a copy that looks similar to the published format.

Confirm your firm's policy regarding article publication. It may be required that a partner review anything in advance of publication.

It is not unusual for a partner to land a writing opportunity and turn to an associate or junior partner to handle the laboring oar. Take advantage of this chance to showcase your knowledge and writing skills. Also, if the partner has a strong reputation with the readership, it will increase the chances of the article being read.

One final note: Be sure to meet your deadline. While an editor may extend the deadline, asking for an extension is not the best way to start a relationship. Editors are usually up against their own deadlines with a print run scheduled and not movable. Your extension puts pressure on the editor's time.

## Speaking/Presentations

*Key Objective:* Demonstrate your expertise.

Speaking is often noted as the primary activity upon which a buying decision is made. It provides the buyer with an opportunity to see if you are indeed knowledgeable and also provides the opportunity for the buyer to see if he/she likes your style and perceives a fit between your performance and his/her legal needs.

The theory behind selecting speaking engagements is the same as for articles: Your target audience should be potential clients and the topic needs to be of current interest to the group. Start with local or regional groups to gain some platform skills and confidence. Look at professional organizations that have monthly meetings with speakers and approach a member of the organization or the program chair. Large national organizations begin putting together the agenda for their annual conferences the day the current conference ends and require the submission of extensive proposals.  Review relevant organizations' websites for more information about speaking opportunities.

In some cases, the way to the podium is through sponsorships and if that is the case, then you will need to coordinate funding with your in-house resources.

Speaking should not be viewed as stand-alone brand development. Look at using the material you prepared as the source for an article or podcast, or consider publishing your PowerPoint or a written summary of your presentation on the firm's website.

## Media/Publicity

*Key Objective:* Use media/publicity wisely.

Without a doubt, your firm has some guidelines with regard to communication with the media. Most likely, the firm expects that all calls from the media be routed to individuals identified as media contacts—partners, its PR firm, or marketing personnel. Your role in media and publicity for the firm is to make certain that any news you have, such as appointment to a board or receiving an award, is shared with the media. While some attorneys have developed a positive professional brand by serving as an expert commentator with media outlets, it tends to be a rare situation. Members of the media have their own priorities, and attorneys are often disappointed by the quotes or comments attributed to them by reporters. In addition, clients must be consulted before comments are made about a case or situation that relates to their interests.

## Firm Committees/Events

*Key Objective:* Pursue internal business development.

Firm committees—whether ad hoc for events or as part of the firm's organizational structure—provide the opportunity to work with a broad range of attorneys, including those you may not otherwise get to meet in the usual course of doing business. Take advantage of the opportunity to build a positive internal brand for yourself by expressing your interest to firm leadership about getting involved in relevant firm committees or activities. Don't be passive and sit back, waiting to be invited to participate. The same guidelines as noted for community and professional organizations hold for internal committee work: Be on time to meetings, demonstrate interest and enthusiasm, and don't miss deadlines. Use your involvement as a way to develop relationships and profile with key colleagues who may later include you in new projects, sales events, and other career-building opportunities.

## Networking/Socializing

*Key Objective:* Broaden your network of business friends and project a positive and helpful brand.

For many attorneys, networking is the cornerstone of all business development efforts. If you enjoy networking or view it as important to developing your connections and brand, then it is important to do it intentionally and not as a random act of marketing. The purpose of networking is to get to know people in your relevant target markets and to develop an influential reputation with them. The process begins by identifying individuals and opportunities you wish to pursue; this relates to your prior identification of relevant target markets and key contacts.

Before a networking event, review the attendance list and consider goals you may have with respect to specific attendees, such as making certain you introduce yourself. If the event is local, familiarize yourself with current issues since they may be the topic of discussion during the session. Make certain you have business cards and that they are easily accessible to you throughout the event. At the event, keep in mind that the last people you want to talk with are those you already know. Make it your mission to meet new people by setting a goal—somewhere between three and five people. Prepare some open-ended questions in advance. If you make a commitment (e.g., "Let's have lunch" or "I will send you that article"), make a note on the person's business card and follow through within two days. A timely follow-up speaks to your organizational skills and interest.

**Social Media**

*Key Objective:* Embrace this aspect of business development, and use it to expand your network and project your brand.

As social media became more pervasive in the business world, organizations quickly developed guidelines for usage. Familiarize yourself with your firm's policy regarding social media and adhere to any rules that might exist. The policy may have been written early on in the development of social media. If you have questions or concerns or you believe the policy is overly restrictive, find someone in the firm to talk to about revamping the policy. Considering the pace of social media's expansion and evolution, it may be outdated.

One of the initial steps to take is to develop a strong profile on LinkedIn. Very few firms have a restriction on posting a profile on LinkedIn; some may even require or strongly encourage it. Creating a LinkedIn profile is not something you should expect your marketing team or your personal assistant to do for you. You might ask for assistance in creating the best possible content, focusing on the key items of title, geography, and summary. The rest of the profile information is easier to complete, especially if you have been managing your professional biography well. You can cut and paste portions over to your LinkedIn profile. After your profile is posted, you need to give serious time and consideration to linking to key connections, striving for quality not quantity. One of the key values of LinkedIn is using it to see who knows whom. When you target a person/company as part of your business development plan, you can use LinkedIn to see if any of your contacts are linked to that target. On the other side of the LinkedIn connection, someone may contact you to seek an introduction to one of your contacts. That networking activity is also important. You can also use LinkedIn as a personal website of sorts, posting updates on your professional activities and links to articles you have written.

The outreach capabilities of social media, including blogging and tweeting, are endless but operate under basic guidelines: Know your firm's policies, and don't start a blog unless you are going to stick with it. Don't tweet if you are not going to be responsive and monitor traffic.

Using the information you collected throughout Chapter Eight, a single Brand Management Matrix worksheet is provided for you to complete as you take charge of building a reputation and brand that will support your efforts to build business.

To avoid so-called "random acts of marketing," provide a description of the profile-raising goal you are seeking to achieve by participating in each specific promotional activity your include on your Matrix. In addition, consider how much non-billable time you have or will invest annually in the activity or event. Focus, too, on how valuable the activity is for achieving brand- and business-building goals. It's important to gauge whether the time investment you make is worth the value to your business development efforts. Finally, describe some specific strategies or actions you will take to maximize the impact of your involvement in an activity or event. Keep in mind that the best business developers find ways to "repurpose" their various promotional activities in order to increase the return on investment of time and effort.

## Professional/Industry Organizations

| ACTIVITY | GOAL(S) | TIME/VALUE | STRATEGIES/ACTION |
|---|---|---|---|
| | | | |
| | | | |
| | | | |
| | | | |

## Community Groups

| ACTIVITY | GOAL(S) | TIME/VALUE | STRATEGIES/ACTION |
|---|---|---|---|
| | | | |
| | | | |
| | | | |
| | | | |

## Speaking Engagements/Presentations

| ACTIVITY | GOAL(S) | TIME/VALUE | STRATEGIES/ACTION |
|---|---|---|---|
| | | | |
| | | | |
| | | | |
| | | | |

Brand Management Matrix

## Articles/Publications

| ACTIVITY | GOAL(S) | TIME/VALUE | STRATEGIES/ACTION |
|----------|---------|------------|-------------------|
|          |         |            |                   |
|          |         |            |                   |
|          |         |            |                   |

## Firm Committees/Events

| ACTIVITY | GOAL(S) | TIME/VALUE | STRATEGIES/ACTION |
|----------|---------|------------|-------------------|
|          |         |            |                   |
|          |         |            |                   |
|          |         |            |                   |

## Social Media

| ACTIVITY | GOAL(S) | TIME/VALUE | STRATEGIES/ACTION |
|----------|---------|------------|-------------------|
|          |         |            |                   |
|          |         |            |                   |
|          |         |            |                   |

## EPILOGUE

# Keep Charging

• • • • • • • •

According to the dictionary, the "epilogue" of a book focuses on the future of the characters and what lies ahead for them based on the actions they have taken to date.

If you have taken the actions described in the *Practical Workbook* and commit to continuing to practice the science and the art of business development as part of your day-to-day work, here are a few of the career developments that you have to look forward to:

- Enduring and mutually beneficial client relationships that provide the type of work you enjoy with clients who value your services
- An increasingly profitable book of business that provides a sustaining flow of work for you and your client service team members
- A sense of control over the future of your practice despite changes in the environmental variables that you can't control
- Becoming a business development role model for your colleagues, and someone who is "additive" to the firm's practice and its bottom line
- Confidence in your own ability to build business now and into the future

And as you master the skills and behaviors described in the *Practical Workbook*, you'll be in a position to move on to understand and integrate a higher level of professional and business development skills, including leading a group business development effort, coaching colleagues in the best practices for building business, and developing innovative service offerings and pricing options to address clients' ever-changing needs. In the words of Thomas Friedman, you will become one of the "new untouchables."

Keep charging ahead to take greater ownership of your career by committing yourself to learn more about and to practice business development as part of each day's work. I welcome your feedback and comments on the ideas expressed in the *Practical Workbook*. Please contact me at mkaczmarek@skillfulmeansmarketing.com.

**Mary Carmel Kaczmarek, Esq.**

# Acknowledgements

• • • • • • •

When smart, motivated professionals come together in a creative effort, they always outperform what an individual can achieve. *The Practical Business Development Workbook* represents the experience, creativity and intelligence of many of my colleagues and my clients, and it is so much better for their input.

First, I thank the following friends and colleagues sincerely for taking the time to engage with me in review and discussion of the book content, and for sharing their time and talents with me and my readers:

***Garza Baldwin, Esq***. – my executive coach and friend, who provided excellent feedback on the manuscript and moral support throughout the process

***Erica Anne de Flamand*** – her artistic talent is reflected in the layout and design of the *Workbook*

***Tim Henderson, Esq.***– for the idea to create the *Workbook*

***Beth Howard*** – my editor, friend and cheerleader extraordinaire

***Blake Raynor*** – creator of the video training modules, and a unique talent and rising star

Second, to the colleagues and clients who reviewed the manuscript and provided excellent feedback (which led to many important revisions): ***Emily Berning, Esq.; Honey Campagna; Silvia Hodges, Esq.; Jill Huse; Lori Reese Patton, Esq.; and Ann Rainhart, Esq.***

Finally, special and sincere thanks to my friend and colleague ***Cathy Petryshyn***, without whose skilled assistance every step of the way this work would have remained a pipe dream.